Flexing Interculturality

This book continues the two scholars' endeavours for opening up more spaces for alternative perspectives, analyses and praxis in interculturality.

The main text features fragments that bear relevance to a wide range of topics including education, politics, personal experiences, social realities, hierarchies, self-critique, language and locus of enunciation. The book takes a step forward by using fragments as an alternative way of doing research and writing scholarship. The premise here is that fragments are human and they reflect our fleeting, inconsistent and unsystematic production of knowledge that today's scholarship has presented to be linear, structured and aligned. The authors draw on fragments to make their points as forcefully as possible by constructing sentences that destabilize themselves and readers to consider other paths and perspectives. That is, writing otherwise may propel thinking otherwise since the very bases, upon which we push our insights to mould through and by, are shaken and ultimately transcended. The chapters include questions with (temporary) answers as an attempt to induce readers to think for themselves and to move beyond what this book has to offer.

This book will be a great read to scholars and students in the field of interculturality, education and sociology. The authors hope that this book will be seen as a genuine example of de-linking from mainstream writing and thinking conventions about interculturality in communication and education without compromising epistemic depth and nuance.

Hamza R'boul is a research assistant professor in the Department of International Education at the Education University of Hong Kong, Hong Kong. His research interests include intercultural education, (higher) education in the Global South, decolonial endeavours in education, cultural politics of language teaching and postcoloniality. His books include *Intercultural Communication Education and Research: Reenvisioning Fundamental Notions* (Routledge, 2023, with Dervin), and *Postcolonial Challenges to Theory and Practice in ELT and TESOL: Geopolitics of Knowledge and Epistemologies of the South* (Routledge, 2023).

Fred Dervin is Professor of Multicultural Education at the University of Helsinki, Finland. Prof. Dervin specializes in intercultural communication education, the sociology of multiculturalism and international mobilities in education. Exploring the politics of interculturality within and beyond the 'canon' of intercultural communication education research has been one of Dervin's idées fixes in his work over the past 20 years. He has widely published over 170 articles and 80 books in different languages on identity, interculturality and mobility/migration. His latest books published with Routledge also include *The Paradoxes of Interculturality* and *Communicating around Interculturality in Research and Education*.

New Perspectives on Teaching Interculturality
Series Editors:
Fred Dervin *is Professor of multicultural education at the University of Helsinki.*

About the Series
This book series publishes original and innovative single-authored and edited volumes contributing robust, new and genuinely global studies to the exciting field of research and practice of interculturality in education. The series aims to enrich the current objectives of 'doing' and teaching interculturality in the 21st century by problematizing Euro- and Western-centric perspectives and giving a voice to other original and under-explored approaches. The series promotes the search for different epistemologies, cutting-edge interdisciplinarity and the importance of reflexive and critical translation in teaching about this important notion. Finally, *New Perspectives on Teaching Interculturality* serves as a platform for dialogue amongst the global community of educators, researchers, and students.

Teaching Interculturality 'Otherwise'
Edited by Fred Dervin, Mei Yuan and Sude

The Paradoxes of Interculturality
A Toolbox of Out-of-the-box Ideas for Intercultural Communication Education
Fred Dervin

Intercultural Communication Education and Research
Reenvisioning Fundamental Notions
Hamza R'boul, Fred Dervin

Communicating around Interculturality in Research and Education
Fred Dervin

For a full list of titles in this series, visit https://www.routledge.com/New-Perspectives-on-Teaching-Interculturality/book-series/NPTI

Flexing Interculturality

Further Critiques, Hesitations, and Intuitions

Hamza R'boul and Fred Dervin

Routledge
Taylor & Francis Group

LONDON AND NEW YORK

First published 2024
by Routledge
4 Park Square, Milton Park, Abingdon, Oxon OX14 4RN

and by Routledge
605 Third Avenue, New York, NY 10158

Routledge is an imprint of the Taylor & Francis Group, an informa business

© 2024 Hamza R'boul and Fred Dervin

British Library Cataloguing-in-Publication Data
A catalogue record for this book is available from the British Library

ISBN: 978-1-032-60105-2 (hbk)
ISBN: 978-1-032-60201-1 (pbk)
ISBN: 978-1-003-45805-0 (ebk)

DOI: 10.4324/9781003458050

Typeset in Times New Roman
by CodeMantra

Contents

Figures

1 Introduction
Sowing question marks
about and for interculturality

Our hands and eyes should be too busy to work...[1]

A pleasing book is one that sows question marks in abundance.
(Cocteau, 1966: 25)

[Our translation of "Un beau livre, c'est celui qui sème à foison les points d'interrogation".]

While we were finalizing this book, one of us had the opportunity to visit the Yungang Grottoes in North China (Shanxi Province, about 16 kilometres from Datong city). Listed as World Heritage by UNESCO in 2011, the Grottoes are located at the foot of Wuzhou Mountain and extend about one kilometre, with 252 caves, more than 1,000 niches and 51,000 statues (with the tallest measuring 17 metres and the smallest 2 cm). Symbolic of Buddhist cave art in China, the grottoes were cut from the mid-5th century to early 6th century. C.E. Zheng Zhendou summarizes (imperfectly) well the experience of visiting the site:

> The majesty and mightiness of the Yungang Grottoes are unimaginable... each grotto, each statue, each head sculpture, each posture, and even each piece of cloth drape, each fire wheel or pattern is worth lingering, appreciating, observing, scrutinizing, analysing and researching...
> Indeed, the overall structure deserves honor as the largest carving museum. However, even a single grotto, a single cave or a single rock can bring its visitor gentleness, tenderness, kindness and prettiness. They are in a complete layout. Together, they are vigorous and gorgeous; separate, each one is complete and distinct... entering a grotto is like entering a mountain of treasures. The abundance of rare treasures and the beautifulness of landscapes make you feel your hands and eyes are too busy to work.
> (in Huanghui, 2013: 17–18)

DOI: 10.4324/9781003458050-1

Walking around the Grottoes, stepping in and out of the caves, peeking at the niches, one becomes awed, observing the different characters, figures, colours, symbols, forms... One is also amazed by the different artistic styles of different times. All this makes describing the grottoes in detail impossible. It would in fact take (more than?) a lifetime to study the complexities of the one-kilometre stretch of caves and niches, and yet one could never be able to grasp its intricacies.

Reflecting on this experience, one cannot but make a (modest) comparison to global academic and educational engagement with the notion of interculturality – a complex construct that deserves to be treated like 'a mountain of treasures', like the Grottoes, rather than a mere monolith as it has tended to be examined since its inception in our worlds of research and education in the 20th century. Like Zheng Zhendou in front of the grottoes, we feel that 'our hands and eyes are too busy to work' when we *think, unthink* and *rethink* the notion that will interest us in this book.

Answering the questions *What are the Yungang Grottoes? What do they 'do' to you?* would be as problematic and polysemic as putting the (often) asked questions of *What is interculturality? How to 'do' it? What impact does it have on us?* The only valid answers are those that express the impossibility to provide a satisfactory response to these questions and/or that leave (a lot of) space for uncertainty, hesitation and further questioning and answering. The worlds of interculturality are far too broad, at micro-, meso- and macro-levels around the globe, to be encaged.

In a similar vein, talking about Beckett's play *Waiting for Godot* (2006) Françon (2023) reminds us that the writer would get upset every time someone asked him who Godot was – this 'ghost-like' figure that the two characters of the play are waiting for... *in vain.* For Françon (2023), what matters in the title of the play is not the five-letter surname (GODOT) but the idea of 'waiting'. Waiting is the most important aspect of the play and the one to be discussed. We could argue the same for interculturality. In trying to delineate (and bound) interculturality through a question such as 'how do you define interculturality?' the focus should be on *define,* not *interculturality: Who is 'begging' for a definition? Why are we urged to define it? What is the (hidden) agenda of asking for a definition – and usually an isolated one? Whose definition is preferred and why? What ideologies does it contain? How much does it seem to take into account destabilizing/contradicting elements?* And more importantly: *How to make sure that* to define *does not lead to 'caging' interculturality in a solid, 'temper-proof', exclusive and beautified box, leading to hegemonic voices to dominate our thinking?*

This book provides some temporary answers to these 'meta-'questions about interculturality (a notion that is toiled with in many fields of research such as language education, nursing, business), by 'sowing question marks in abundance' to go back to the opening quote by Cocteau. Like the aforementioned grottoes from China, this book presents the reader with an abundance of (limited) 'resources' while telling us that interculturality as a notion must disappoint us – a word based etymologically on the idea of 'reversing' (dis-) having been made ready, arranged and settled (appoint). *Interculturality as disappointment* – interculturality as a complex, contradictory, unfaithful notion that will never satisfy our needs to 'circumscribe', 'define', 'grasp', 'arrange', 'programme' and 'prepare'. *Interculturality as a question rather than a mere (simplistic) answer.*

The book title suggests that we are going to *flex* interculturality in this book. The very verb is reminiscent of and probably a back-formation of today's popular word *flexible.* Figuratively the word originally referred to *tractable* and *inconstant.* We also note the inclusion of the interesting adjective *flexiloquent* in an 18th dictionary which meant 'speaking words of doubtful or double meaning' (etymonline, 2023). When planning the book, we first thought of using the verb *to shatter* (*to break into pieces*) in the title ('Shattering Interculturality') since, as we shall see in a moment, we have adopted a very special form of writing, *fragments* (small separated and yet intertwined pieces of writing), which Fred has launched as a way of enriching takes on interculturality in the broad field of intercultural communication education (Dervin, 2022a,b). However, considering the potential misunderstandings that the verb might lead to in a book title, we have opted for *to flex.* The verb can have two meanings in the English language, which we find stimulating. To flex can mean *to bend repeatedly*, without breaking (a bit like bamboo trees in the wind), *to move or tense by contraction.* In informal English, it might also refer to *talking in boastful or aggressive ways* or *to show off.* The first understanding is what we are trying to do to interculturality in the book (*repeatedly*), while reminding ourselves and our readers of the dangers of 'showing off' about our own (limited and limiting) ways of engaging with the notion. Flexing interculturality *ad infinitum* is also a way for us to "understand that there are things which [human understanding] cannot understand..." (Kierkegaard, 2004: 32).

Listening to György Kurtág's (1963–1968) song cycle *The Sayings of Péter Bornemisza* for soprano and piano while working on this book helped us give meaning to what the complex (and endless) processes of *flexing interculturality* might entail. A very challenging piece for both singer and piano player, the 50-minute song cycle sets words by a Hungarian Lutheran bishop (Péter Bornemisza). Each section of the cycle treats the Sayings, which deal with the trials of faith to redemption, as fragments, throwing us the listeners into varied soundscapes throughout (from quivering on one note to fits of hysterics). If one listens carefully to the piece, one can hear and feel somehow the torments described by the singer herself, who has to navigate complex counterpoint and shifts in dynamic, alternating between e.g., barking fury, wailing grief and breathy despair. For Willson (2003: 315),

> The text is rough and earthy as well as religious, evoking vile horrors of evil and death as emphatically as the longing for redemption. As such,

it provides a powerful vehicle for musical representation, through vocal declamation, imitation of emotional states and iconic allusion.

In her singing the soprano has to flex dynamic, pulse, register and vocal timbre, imitating somehow the complexities of human thoughts, emotions and interdependence and un-balance with (imaginary) others. Our book flexes the very notion of interculturality in similar ways, pulling and pushing it *to and fro*, testing its energies, resistance, incoherence, inconsistencies, contradictions (as well as our own). As much as interculturality is alive and thus uncontrollable, this book represents an attempt to explore the notion closer to these intricate while somehow frustrating but real aspects.

Flexing Interculturality: Further Critiques, Hesitations, and Intuitions also functions the way the artist Jean Dubuffet (2014: n.p.) describes the role of the viewer of art:

> If we make a painting where all the elements are detailed, the viewer has their horizon blocked, their imaginative mechanism does not work. Instead if we give them something a little sketchy, there is a psychological mechanism in them that leads their imagination to function, to supplement things that do not exist in the work of art.[2]

The painting belongs both to the artist and to the viewer. In a similar vein, the following chapters belong to both of us, the authors and you the readers. Together as authors, and in indirect dialogues with readers, we *flex* interculturality in the book, putting our imagination to the test in the process.

The book revolves around three keyworks found in its subtitle: *Further critiques, hesitations* and *intuitions*. These keywords reflect both the modesty and flexing processes that we put into practice. *Critiquing* (or: adding to previous (own) critiques – see our use of *Further* in the subtitle – while being critical of our criticality), *hesitating* about interculturality and having (limited) *intuitions* as to how to move forward and/or pause guide us in exploring different 'treasures' of interculturality. These three elements also send the message that we wish to refrain from 'preaching' about interculturality[3] – a phenomenon that is often found in the literature about interculturality, with 'models of intercultural competence', economic-political 'orders' disguised as scientific/pedagogical approaches (Dervin & Simpson, 2020; Dervin & Yuan, 2022; R'boul & Dervin, 2023).

In order to deal with these challenges, we place language at the centre of our 'question marks' – both working *with* and *against* language; language as a way of looking into ourselves and of communicating with others. Words must be systematically interrogated in the process of flexing. Words in any of the languages that we use to speak about, write about, interact about and listen to discourses of interculturality. An example from Chinese, in an article published in English, is provided here to illustrate this need for some form of *sensitivity* to words:

> (…) It's important to 'de-culturalize' tea to become [just] a tasty beverage," 29-year-old tea blogger surnamed Sun from Nanchang, Jiangxi province, tells TWOC. Sun, who has around 140,000 followers on social media platform Xiaohongshu and goes by her online name of Xingxing, attributes the previous unpopularity of tea among younger consumers to the industry and government emphasizing the cultural aspects of tea, including the recent UNESCO recognition of China's traditional tea processing techniques and associated customs, which may sound "antiquated" and too "heavy and serious" for young consumers.
>
> (Yunfei, 2023)

This was published in 2023 in an online article about Chinese young people's growing interest in tea. Discussing the unpopularity of the tea amongst them, a blogger uses the following words and phrases: (the need to) *'de-culturalize' tea, industry, government*, but also *'antiquated', 'heavy and serious'* – and probably more important: *'young customers'*. Interestingly, although this is about 'tea culture', the blogger pushes for 'de-culturalizing' it by referring only to both the pressure of the industry and the authorities. Culture here seems to have to do with 'money', 'the market' and 'government'. The use of the word *culture*, which is a central term in the notion of interculturality, appears to stand for something else, some kind of 'obvious' and yet 'semi-hidden' agenda – i.e. to make money by selling tea to 'young customers'. Using *culture* instead of *politics* or *money* (as in 'de-politicize' tea; 'de-marketize' tea) appears to be a strategic position that could soften the message of the blogger.

[If one observes carefully discourses of interculturality in global research – our own included – such discursive 'games' are plentiful. Hence the need to flex repeatedly to ensure that we can talk to each other about a polysemic notion like interculturality.]

In the book we practice systematically this awareness of how we formulate things around the *inter-, cultur-* and *-ity* of interculturality, what we seem to be doing with them in the intersection of the market, politics and research, as a way of pushing (imperfectly) things forward with the notion, leading us to open our eyes a little bit more in front of the 'treasures' of the notion, discovering new perspectives, (mis-)uses and practices. Following Leiris (2017: 167), we could refer to this process as trying to *cross the mirror of language*.

Beyond 'humiliated repetition'?

> The bastard form of mass culture is humiliated repetition... always new books, new programs, new films, news items, but always the same meaning.
>
> (Barthes, 2020: 45)

[Hamza: My early readings of interculturality were of those scholars who have rejected the dominant narratives and discourses around differences and essentialism. I managed to develop a critical and doubtful orientation towards ready-made ideas that were waiting to be embraced rather than questioned and critiqued. We should not force notions to explain the world, but rather how the world is always open to re-interpretation and re-theorizing. Notions are possibilities, not certainties, and reality tends to manifest itself through ontological possibilities that generate, unsettle, and pluralize truths in certain times, spaces, and cultures.]

[Fred: My early readings of interculturality were of those scholars who had embraced the dominant narratives and discourses around differences, culturalism and essentialism. It took a long time before I managed to develop a critical and doubtful orientation towards ready-made ideas that were waiting to be embraced rather than questioned and critiqued. I had to swallow in dominating ideologies of the 1980s/1990s before vomiting them to ingurgitate other ideologies that were to become domineering in turn. Pluralizing 'truths' is my only goal today.]

The word *intercultural* (and its companions such as *multicultural* and *transcultural*) is found in thousands of publications about education and communication in English and other languages around the world. Specific perspectives and 'models' related to the notion have spread to all corners of the world, 'conveying' specific ideologies, orders, agendas, windscreens (Roucek, 1944). One day, one speaks of 'democratic culture' (a 'European' substitute for interculturality), another day, 'intercultural citizenship'. These words spread, are recycled, often emptied of their economic-political essence, re-embedded in different (economic-political contexts) and used to 'order', 'examine' but also 'judge' those who 'do' interculturality. In fact, very few variations of *interculturalspeak* are used, especially in global research on the notion (Peng et al., 2019) – perspectives, critiques and epistemologies from the 'Global South' (amongst others) being often ignored and/or silenced im-/ex-plicitly.

Many of the popular and dominating ideologies often seem to serve as distractions. One could find similarities with Aesop's Drowning Boy, where a boy had gone to bathe in a river and as he was drowning, a man who was trying to pull him out of the water scolded him for attempting to enter the water while he had not learnt to swim, to which the boy replied 'Right now I just need your help; you can lecture me about it afterwards!'. The fable reminds us of the inappropriateness and out-of-placeness of criticizing during moments of crisis. *And yes, the world is in crises (plural!).* Interculturality experiences many and varied crises, from concrete encounters to the education and research that try to deal with it. Being reminded constantly from exclusively Eurocentric perspectives of the importance of 'worshipping' e.g. democracy and human rights, but also decolonizing while refraining from positioning these elements clearly from outside dominating ideological contexts, is a distraction that won't make interculturality 'better'. This distraction – which is in fact a form of 'humiliated repetition' as Barthes puts it in the opening quote – silences other ways of thinking, unthinking and rethinking interculturality *ad infinitum.* By serving as mere *blanc-seings* that are already printed on the page we use to write about the notion, this worshipping also prevents us from interculturalizing interculturality (Dervin, 2021; Dervin & Jacobsson, 2022), this important way of treating *interculturality interculturally*, opening up constantly to contradictions, disagreements, revisions, ideological clashes, etc. While our book does not demand shunning the available literature, we are seeking to incite readers to exercise constant appraisal of what they know and why they came to know certain things in certain ways. We think that distancing the self a bit from 'usual' discourses can allow us to develop a more perceptive account of what interculturality may be to other people – and then in a mirror-process to self *again and again.*

Our book thus represents another attempt at dealing with 'humiliated repetitions' about interculturality. Although the reader will identify repetitions in it (which is unavoidable), the writing form that we have adopted, which accepts some of the elements listed in the previous paragraphs (contradictions, disagreements, etc.), allows us to revise, add to (temporarily) and even discard them. We have cooperated on two books before this one (Dervin & R'boul, 2022; R'boul & Dervin, 2023[4]) and *Flexing Interculturality* represents a 'logical' addition to our cooperation, pushing our exploration of interculturality to the limits. In Dervin and R'boul (2022), we got acquainted with each other's work and personal-academic experiences as two scholars from very different contexts (Morocco, Finland). This first book is an important starting point in laying down epistemic, ethical and interpersonal foundations for working on interculturality from our different contexts, making our cooperation closer to an idea of interculturality that aims for (constant) co-construction and co-revision of the notion in education and communication. In R'boul and Dervin (2023), we toil through a selected number of concepts that are made use of in relation to interculturality in the literature. We also proposed a certain number of concepts that we feel can support us in expanding our takes on the notion. While this last book was being written, we challenged each other to write down fragments every day for a period of 7 months, which would serve as a basis for *Flexing Interculturality*.

Fragments as interculturality – interculturality as fragments

Since 2020, as said earlier, Fred has developed the habit of writing a fragment about interculturality per day in a notebook and/or drawing to summarize, problematize, question an idea he had come across and/or thought of by himself. Many philosophers, thinkers and writers have made use of fragments in their writing (e.g. Canetti, 1989; Cioran, 1992; Lichtenberg, 2000). In 2022 Fred published two collections of fragments to share his 'findings' with international audiences. In Dervin (2022a), he explains that fragments are "form(s) of creative nonfiction, which look(s) like 'notes'" (Dervin, 2022a: 3), which "represent attempts to put knowledge in a nutshell" (Dervin, 2022a: 4) while staying in our mind, leading to new ideas or simply disappearing. For him, fragment writing for interculturality serves three purposes (Dervin, 2022a: 3):

(1) To expose the complexity of reflecting on interculturality as both a phenomenon and an object of research and education, especially within a long-term period (a year); (2) To give access to a scholar's inner thoughts, ideologies and contradictions about the way the notion is discussed in research, (social) media and daily life in different parts of the world; (3) To offer support to the reader to treat interculturality in a fragment perspective, urging them to unthink and rethink it, and, like me (imperfectly), to expand their critical and reflexive abilities.

Fragment writing appears to be well fitted to reflect on interculturality; this complex phenomenon that has no real beginning, no real end; this complex phenomenon that is always in-between and creative; this complex phenomenon that is always 'fleeting' and fragmentary. We are not always aware of these phenomena and we argue that fragments remind us that our engagements with the notion of interculturality are never straightforward and that we need to be even more flexible than we might usually be in front of it. The fragments in this book thus represent "a sum, see a jigsaw, of thoughts" (Dervin, 2022a: 5) which reveal our own (at times overlapping) struggles and contradictions when we consider interculturality through our own research, readings, experiences, encounters, artistic experiences, etc. We discuss with ourselves, (sometimes openly) with others, we dis-/agree with what we read and hear, we question word use and ideologies, we revise our thoughts, we share our frustrations and disbeliefs, we identify and recognize our contradictions... The personal is often found in our fragments since we do not believe that writing about interculturality as scholars and intellectuals should 'hide' what we do outside the spheres of a computer or a lecture hall. Interculturality is not something that can be experienced as we wish, in specific times and places. *It is always here and there...* All in all, the fragments reveal both our (complex) humanity and interculturality and do not pretend that we are following a straight line, 'rationalizing' interculturality. We *triturate* (a verb that meant originally *grinding into powder*) our/others' thoughts, impressions, words, ideologies, injustices… We do contradict ourselves in the process; we do try out new ideas and (sometimes) revise them. This will feel destabilizing for some readers but we ask you to be patient, to listen to us while thinking and dialoguing with us. Accepting our own contradictions and hesitations is central in intercultural communication education. Working upon them – not necessarily to transform them or to find a 'Truth' – represents another important goal. This is why the flexing of interculturality in this book does not offer any solution or direction to issues of interculturality in research and education (note the singular) but *solutions* and *directions*, which are (to be) in turn re-interrogated. In general, we do believe that the fragments included in the book are not only strongly related to the attempt of reconceptualizing interculturality but they also suggest casting off the (colonial) baggage of concepts, notions, ideologies, methods, exercising caution in using them to empty their ideological implications and re-shaping them to be used by us rather than just being at the receiving end of the indoctrination they often represent.

Let us pause for a moment to listen to Hamza's reactions to fragment writing:

Writing these fragments allowed me to witness the fragmentation of human geographies of reason. The pressure for rationality, relationality, dynamicity, pattern and systematicity in academic writing may not accurately represent the lack of organization, unpredictability and eccentricity of the human mind. The western cognitive empire has framed and conditioned us to dismiss any form of knowledge production that is not linear or sequential. The way we think does not organically translate into our writings since they are refined, measured and mannered. Our reasonings are spiral, going up and down, left and right, to and fro without clear structure or regulation. We only write what is politically correct in terms of how knowledge is supposed to look like and how narratives should be arranged as dictated by dominant western traditions of thought.

Fragments supply a feeling of freedom. It is the liberty from academic stringent criteria and guidelines to write and think in certain ways. It is refreshing to 'jump' and 'navigate' various positions and insights without having to be linear and organized. Fragmentation is human and it is more faithful to our thoughts although writing systematically is again a constitutive dimension in refining our ideas since it forces structure and clarity.

We fully understand that some colleagues might have concerns over the use of "fragments" for 'testing' and 'adding to' knowledge about interculturality. For example, one of the reviewers of this book project used the (negative) word "amalgamated" to refer to what we are doing in the book. Many scholars having written about this special (and unique) genre (at least for the complex field of interculturality) do describe the reticence and potentially negative perceptions of fragment-writing by scholars used to typical 'Western' 'scientific' writing (see e.g., Elias, 2021). Using fragment-writing and accompanying explanatory metatexts, we hope to foreground the non-linear trajectories that humans are engaged in while producing knowledge. We think that "fragments", despite the unfavourable perception that they might be "unscientific", "unsystematic" and "unconventional", are true representations of the workings of the human mind – and thus of interculturality as a *changeable, fluid* and *power-laden* type of construction. We do think that the current literature on interculturality (even its so-called 'critical strand') represents a vast body of scholarship that employs conventional methodologies and traditions of thought. In this book, the very premise is *writing otherwise culminating in thinking otherwise*, thus hoping to offer readers a new way of reading and imagining knowledge. Fragments are raw, direct and unpolished to make sense and connect to others ideas. Fragments may have a strong impact as they are intense and condensed chunks of knowledge.

Flexing the (negative) aforementioned idea of "amalgamated", one might hypothesize that readers can enjoy reading two books *within* this one. Instead of fusing our fragments to deliver the false assumption that we think and write the same way, we would like to tell readers that we are two people driven by the same rationale of decentring and disrupting but who do not necessarily speak, write and think the same way. This ensures somehow that none of us is melting into the other, but 'being melted' by the readers allowing themselves to experience more epistemological excitement by having two *reads within one*, two *'knowledgings' within one* and *two 'thinkings' within one* – with all these overlapping and yet distancing themselves at times. These processes do resemble what interculturality could be about in the reality of daily interactions. With the book, we are thus showing how these (intercultural) dis-connecting and balancing processes should also occur in academic writing – rather than 'façading' (Western imposed) logic, rationality, objectivity, one-sided criticality...

Empowering readers to experience and try out other ways of writing and dealing with interculturality beyond the dominating 'Westerncentric' modes of knowledge production is an important goal, since readers are ignored in most publications about the notion.

Finally, we would like to note that this book endeavours to *liberate* rather than *circumscribe*. Liberation here accounts for the very needed emancipation of the mind from the very shackles of 'rigor' within theory and methodology as dictated by 'Western' epistemologies. That is following the same traditions of writing, thinking and doing research would belie our attempts at *decentring* (a principle to which many of us seem to be attached today). The problematic here is *why would we critique the unconventional by flagging how unconventional it is?* in the sense that we do not treat the unconventional as a nonderivative approach in itself. Instead we make use of the conventional to "look at" and "see" the non-conventional. We hope this would liberate our readers to take the initiative to think, write and do methodology *otherwise*. The current world situations are calling for urgent changes in the way we 'do', conceptualize and ideologize interculturality. Although we do not consider ourselves 'activists', we do believe that a book like this one, in dialogue with the ones we have already co-written, can contribute modestly to push for change.

How to use the book

It is important to say at the outset that the book requires 'familiarity' with some of today's knowledge about the notion of interculturality so it is not meant to be used as e.g. an introductory book. What 'some of today's knowledge' means here is difficult to circumscribe since interculturality is embedded in many different fields of knowledge and taught/researched in varied ways in different languages around the world. However, based on our experiences of teaching and researching interculturality in different parts of the world and in a (limited) range of languages, we are aware that there is some globally dominating knowledge (mostly produced in and flavoured ideologically by some parts of the 'West') about interculturality (see e.g. Peng et al., 2019). We do refer to such knowledge as often as we can in the book.

Over a period of seven months we each wrote about 300 fragments. Each fragment contains between 10 and 250 words. Having read all of them together, we then 'categorized' them into three chapters: *Critiques and mysteries*; *Hesitations and doubts* and *Further intuitions*. The themes covered in the fragments are multifaceted but revolve around (amongst others) *academia, the arts, decolonial, the economic, internationalization, language use, the political, teaching-learning*. While reading the fragments several times concurrently, we realized that some of our individual fragments complemented each other, and that others resembled each other. Interestingly, after organizing them in the sections it often appeared impossible to determine who wrote what (we have decided not to add our names for each fragment to let the reader decide for themselves whose fragment they are reading – should they wish to 'play this game'). For the seven months that we were writing the fragments, we communicated freely on a daily basis via the Chinese social media application WeChat, which is somewhat equivalent to 'Western' social media apps such as WhatsApp or even Facebook. Some of these conversations can also be felt in the fragments since we refer to each other's voices from this extra layer of discourse. At the time of putting the fragments together, we also added comments on some of the fragments between brackets. All in all, the principle of 同心协力 (*working together with one heart*) was practiced in writing *Flexing Interculturality* and we recommend adopting this principle in more research on interculturality. As much as we are pushing for the 'critical' as a filter through which the un-critical is re-thought, we may need to probe into what one of us has referred to as *the criticality of our criticality* (Dervin, 2022a) and the parameters through which we determine the criticality of one discourse and not another. This is something we explore in this book as well.

Each chapter starts with an introduction and is divided into a certain number of subsections. At the end of each chapter, we have added a list of ten terms from the fragments that we find essential as takeaways. 'Temporary' definitions for each of them are provided, hoping that we can come back to them in future publications and urging readers to complement these definitions. We have also added five questions for the reader to reflect on at the end of each chapter as well as a short conclusion.

Some of the fragments are self-explanatory while others might require more interpretative work from the reader. This is on purpose to allow your imagination and curiosity 'for more' to be activated. If you have ever seen (valuable) Ancient Chinese calligraphies you might have noticed that many red seals have been applied to them. These are from previous owners of these 'works of art' who have placed their names or mottoes on them to show that they are part of *the history of the calligraphies*. We do encourage you to do the same with our fragments. Place your own 'marks' *on, above, in* and *between* our fragments on interculturality. They belong to you as much as they belong to us – as asserted earlier when we considered Dubuffet's ideas.

The book can be read chapter after chapter or in a completely random order. You might for instance open the book at any page and read any fragment to reflect on. The book is meant to be 'digested' slowly and should be read as often as possible. It can also be considered as a book for finding inspiration for *flexing* interculturality as an object of research and education. We do hope that you will disagree with many of our ideas, arguments and interpretations and that they will push you to think further about the notion (re-reading the fragments several times while preparing the final manuscript, we did disagree with what we had written some months ago).

[*Cocteau's (1966: 4) advice about reading is inspiring here*:

I read. I think I am reading. Each time I re-read, I perceive that I have not read. (…) If they [books] do not suit our present mood we do not consider them good. If they disturb us, we criticize them, and this criticism is superimposed upon them and prevents us from reading them fairly. What the reader wants is to read himself (sic). When he reads what he approves of he thinks he could have written it. He may even have a grudge against the book for taking his place, for saying what he did not know how to say, and which according to him he would have said better. The more a book means to us the less well we read it. Our substance slips into it and thinks it round to our own outlook. That is why if I want to read and convince myself that I can read, I read books into which my substance does not penetrate.]

The book is divided into five chapters, including this introduction and a conclusion. Chapter 2, *Critiques and mysteries*, focuses on deep lacerations within research as a political activity. It particularly encircles the subtle dynamics including our practices and use of words that implicitly orient our epistemological stances to endorse certain ideologies and not others. While a number of insights may sound unnecessarily censorious, the overriding rationale is to induce some discomfort that would eventually yield substantial (un)learning and (re)thinking. Chapter 2 invites us to exercise constant re-appraisal of our readings of others and enunciations of ourselves so as to gradually alleviate our blurry imaginations of knowledge construction, dissemination and consumption around interculturality and other topics. *Hesitations and doubts* (Chapter 3) relates to the scholar's and educator's fundamental apparatuses for ceasing the recycling of our own situated knowledges and questioning the extent to which our discourses are not self-serving. Instead of continuing to project an aura of refusing to stretch back to witness more horizons, Chapter 3 exposes our loci of enunciation for unravelling the types of contradictions, reconciliations and aspirations that are interlocked within our texts to speak about interculturality. Throughout the chapter, we question without the burden of providing cogent answers. We also engage in self-critique to model a healthy approach for crystallize the type of epistemic doubting that could further refine our intellectual labour about interculturality and other topics. The questions asked by the chapter are meant to destabilize our reasonings to allow for some refreshing crevices. Chapter 4 introduces further intuitions. The English word *intuition* comes from Latin for *a looking at, consideration* (the Proto-Indo European root *tueri* for *to look at* and *watch over* relates to the Latin stem). This chapter adds to the previous ones by putting forward a certain number of (provisional) proposals and hypotheses about what interculturality could be about and aim at in education and research. This endless sharpening of our thinking occurs through the use of metaphors and by discussing some contradictions in the way we have been made to think, unthink and rethink interculturality. Stimulation to adopt and practice lateral thinking about interculturality is used as an (imperfect) way to face, accept and indulge somewhat in some of these contradictions. The chapter also shares some of our intuitions concerning language use in problematizing interculturality, enriching it and caring about it *linguistically*. The autobiographical comes back at the end of the chapter to add to the intuitive tone of the chapter. Finally, a conclusion helps the reader 'collect' takeaways and their own thoughts about the endless process of *flexing interculturality* in research and education.

This book, based on fragments written separately by the authors but combined in different chapters reiterates the exigency of looking elsewhere to move forward with and for interculturality. Each fragment and the peritexts around them (comments from authors, references to other scholars, indirect dialogues with readers) is meant to be treated like each of the hundreds of caves and niches of the Yungang Grottoes mentioned at the beginning of this chapter. They each work separately and yet relate and form an interrelated network of thoughts.

These chunks of knowledge are condensed and deliver fractions of our social realities with unlimited scope of expansion and elaboration by the readers themselves. These fragments are not absolute knowledges but rather urge readers to taste their promptness and sharpness to make sense, process and produce more detailed knowledge. The fragments that compose this book are also possibilities for doing research on interculturality and other topics *otherwise* (R'boul, 2022). Thinking *otherwise* may be further reinforced by writing *otherwise* in ways that encourage structuring our insights according to manners, intonation and tones that do not necessarily abide by mainstream conventions. These fragments are not only alternative ways of drawing scholarship but also alternative paths of thinking and researching within interculturality and other fields.

Notes

1 This introduction is not meant to *define* or *anti-define* interculturality but to present the two authors' working principles for this special book and to pave the way for what is coming in the central chapters that *flex, bend, activate* and *move* the notion *in all directions*. The issue of defining (or not defining) interculturality as a first entry into a book is further problematized to avoid misunderstandings and to counter (typical 'rational', 'objectivizing') expectations of e.g. *a method* or *anti-method, schools of praxis*, in a book that aims to 'test' the notion of interculturality to its limits.

2 Our translation of "si on fait un tableau où tous les éléments sont détaillés, le spectateur de ce tableau a son horizon bouché, son mécanisme imaginatif ne fonctionne pas. Au lieu que si on lui donne quelque chose d'un peu sommaire, il se produit un mécanisme psychologique chez lui qui entraine son imagination à fonctionner, à suppléer aux choses qui n'existent pas sur le tableau".

3 One of the reviewers for this book referred to this book as 'activism'. We note that we do not consider our work as that of 'activists' but as a simple contribution to renewing (our) thinking (endlessly) with readers. Although many ideas shared in the book are anchored in some form of politics (in the broad sense of the word), we ask for, accept and wish to reflect further on the (critical) content of the arguments that we develop in the chapters.

4 The use of 'heavy' self-citation in this introductory chapter reflects the 'heavy' global contribution of the two authors (and that of their network) over the past years and especially of the very influential and special work of the second author on the notion of interculturality for 25 years. We note that 'self-citation' here also has to do with contextualizing this book in relation to the two other ones that we have already published and with our principle of 'criticality of criticality' – not being merely satisfied with our previous scholarship but enhancing it again and again – and often failing to contribute anything 'new' or 'fresh'. We obviously do refer to tens of other (influential) scholars in the fragments and other metatexts in what follows.

References

Barthes, R. (2020). *Roland Barthes*. London: Vintage Classics.

Beckett, S. (2006). *Waiting for Godot*. London: Faber & Faber.

Canetti, E. (1989). *The Secret Heart of the Clock: Notes, Aphorisms, Fragments*. New York: Farrar, Straus and Giroux.

Cioran, E. M. (1992). *Anathemas and Admirations*. New York: Quartet Books.

Cocteau, J. (1966). *Difficulty of Being*. London: Peter Owen Publishers.

Dervin, F. (2021). Critical and Reflexive Languaging in the Construction of Interculturality as an Object of Research and Practice (19 April 2021). Digital series of talks on plurilingualism and interculturality, University of Copenhagen.

Dervin, F. (2022a). *Intercultural in Fragments: A Reflexive Approach*. Singapore: Springer.

Dervin, F. (2022b). *The Paradoxes of Interculturality*. London: Routledge.

Dervin, F., & Jacobsson, A. (2022). *Intercultural Communication Education: Broken Realities and Rebellious Dreams*. Singapore: Springer.

Dervin, F., & R'boul, H. (2022). *Through the Looking-Glass of Interculturality. Auto-Critiques*. Singapore: Springer.

Dervin, F., & Simpson, A. (2020). *Interculturality and the Political Within Education*. London: Routledge.

Dervin, F., & Yuan, M. (2022). Political ideology and atonality in language and intercultural education: A rejoinder to 'Between professionalism and political engagement in foreign language teaching practice' by Claire Kramsch. *Journal of Applied Linguistics and Professional Practice*, *16*(3), 31–45.

Dubuffet, J. (2014). Des idees et des hommes – quelques propos sur la peinture. *France Culture*. https://www.radiofrance.fr/franceculture/podcasts/les-nuits-de-france-culture/des-idees-et-des-hommes-quelques-propos-sur-la-peinture-7772436

Elias, C. (2021). *The Fragment: Towards a History and Poetics of a Performative Genre*. New York: EyeCorner Press.

Etymonline (2023). Flex. https://www.etymonline.com/search?q=flex

Françon, A. (2023). Les personnages de Beckett bossent dur pour nous. *France Culture*. https://www.radiofrance.fr/franceculture/podcasts/par-les-temps-qui-courent/alain-francon-metteur-en-scene-8048300

Huanghui, N. (2013). *Yungang Grottoes and Northern Wei*. Beijing: China Intercontinental Press.

Kierkegaard, S. (2004). *Either/Or. A Fragment of Life*. London: Penguins.

Leiris, M. (2017). *Fibrils*. New Haven, CT & London: Yale University Press.

Lichtenberg, G. (2000). *The Waste Books*. New York: New York Review Books.

Peng, R.-Z., Zhu, C., & Wu, W.-P. (2019). Visualizing the knowledge domain of intercultural competence research: A bibliometric analysis. *International Journal of Intercultural Relations*, 74, 58–68.

R'boul, H. (2022). Afterword: Theorising and teaching interculturality otherwise: What 'otherwise'? In F. Dervin, M. Yuan, & N.A. Sude (Eds.), *Teaching Interculturality 'Otherwise'* (pp. 222–226). London: Routledge.

R'boul, H., & Dervin, F. (2023). *Intercultural Communication Education and Research: Reenvisioning Fundamental Notions*. London: Routledge.

Roucek, J. S. (1944). A history of the concept of ideology. *Journal of the History of Ideas*, 5(4), 479–488.

Willson, R. B. (2003). To Say and/or To Be? Imcongruence in Kurtág's *The Sayings of Péter* Bornemisza, Op. 7. *Music Analysis*, 22(iii), 315–338.

Yunfei, T. (2023). Tea total: Is China's new social media-fueled tea craze more than just a fad? *The World of Chinese*. February 2023. https://www.theworldofchinese.com/2023/02/tea-total-is-chinas-new-social-media-fueled-tea-craze-more-than-just-a-fad/

2 Critiques and mysteries

Introduction

This chapter establishes critiques as a priori for transcending what we know. That is, dismantling and dissecting the mainstream locate the cracks and fissures that allow scholars and readers to transgress the 'coloniatellectual' boundaries, unsettle and interrupt the power they exert so as to resurge from the margins. Mysteries are presented as areas of thought where epistemology and logics are struggling to explain what is intimately convoluted. The fragments are asking intense questions that may prompt the readers to question how, why and what interculturality is about. The fragments are not necessarily harmonious and euphonic but they glean various epistemological tastes and angles of observing and analysing. As a whole, this chapter is about looking elsewhere as it doubts the very essence of the major topics that the authors have been working on, especially our crusading stances. This chapter thus refuses to rehearse that science and knowledge production is about addressing *the gap*. Instead, it argues that *the gap itself is not a gap per se*, but rather a deviation from what the dominant has designated as *a gap*. Instead of zooming into the gap, we may need to doubt the perspectives, knowledges and understandings that have hypothetically created, legitimized and accentuated that gap. The gap is not an end itself but rather a political manoeuvre to shackle epistemic beings and circumscribe their epistemological ambits.

Eight subsections compose the chapter: [The "international" as a smoke-screen to deviate], [Decolonial neurosis], [Research and interculturality: disconnection from reality], [Words write us], [The 'critical': a new opium], [Miscellaneous critiques], [Fantasizing interculturality] and ['Orders' about interculturality]. [Decolonial neurosis] is questioning the underpinnings of decolonial discourses as a site of cognitive dissonance where one is enunciating for the sake of 'sounding' rather than 'doing'. [Research and interculturality: disconnection from reality] interrogates what we tend to claim and how our knowledge of interculturality does not yield a sufficient ability to navigate intercultural encounters. We share our stories of interculturality and how we problematize our own sense of what interculturality could be.

DOI: 10.4324/9781003458050-2

[The 'critical': a new opium] unpacks how criticality is an analgesic buzzword in the field used to canvass succour while it may repudiate and reenact the very dominant trajectories but in different forms and shapes. The chapter concludes with some questions for the readers to continue the tradition of starting from the critique of the ethos of interculturality to fall into mysteries and ultimately rise to the horizons.

[The "international" as a smokescreen to deviate]

247[1]

Internationalization, in essence, is a potential structural remedy to some contexts' subalternity and ostensible lack of academic and scientific rigour. That is, instead of publicly declaring that they need foreign expertise to ameliorate their educational systems and universities, they clutch 'internationalization' as a framework and euphemism that can ensure the same objectives but with a lot of sugar-coating and covering.

246

Internationalization and its skewed geopolitics of knowledge and movement is a genuine example of power asymmetries and imbalanced interculturality.

[Institutions and individual academics tend to associate with 'international' peers and institutions of the same 'calibre' to project a specific identity of 'internationalization'.]

245

The internationalization of higher education entails a large-scale movement of scholars from the Global South. To 'shine', it is necessary to be based at a Northern university and to be associated with Northern scholars, institutions and structures. Southern scholars are, thus, required to move out of their home countries in order to ensure a more promising future as an academic. The fact that one has to leave family and friends, and go to places that they may not like or not be able to fit in/adapt to is a complex challenge. We may exude the impression that scholars are invincible and independent but they remain human beings who need a support system to function. Families and friends are important and they are a fundamental part of scholars' lives, irrespective of one's status, talent and experience.

244

Interculturality as a capitalist entry: I pretend to be your 'international colleague-friend'; I am nice to you; I make you believe that you have become one of us; I manipulate you; I hide things from you since you don't understand 'our' language. *However,* I cheat on you; I abuse your hard work; I fool everyone around us about our strong friendship and cooperation; I hide your name from sight. Most of all I collect points on your back to get promoted, to try to make a name for myself and, in the end, make a financial profit. *I still play your friend. I don't think that you know what game I am playing.*

243

Politics of distraction are hindering the Global South from moving forward. In Morocco, for instance, all political discoursers tend to foreground the marginal and the temporary when the core issues are sidelines because addressing them entails restricting the privilege and the impunity of some people. In education, scholars and citizens have been convinced that embracing English instead of French (the ex-colonial code) will solve all educational problems. A lot of countries have English as a first or second language, but that has not automatically translated into a quality educational system. English could be a factor but it is not an elixir that would radically improve everything for the better. Politicians overlook how much money is allocated for trivial matters such as festivals. Instead of taking a bold stance, and investing more in education, they would propagate some misleading "claims" about how Moroccan universities have moved up in international rankings.

242

Politicized interculturality underscores the necessity that we bring ourselves to engage, question and critique all knowledges that claim internationality and that they know what suits us better than ourselves per se. It also addresses the possibility that our knowledges and epistemologies that we purport to be decentred, alternative and southern may be still western.

241

At Beijing Olympics, transfer taxis were equipped with AI translation machines to speak to the drivers. A European participant refused to use one of these machines and insisted on speaking to the driver in English. The latter did not understand a word of the lingua franca. "This driver is stupid!", shouted the European at a Chinese volunteer. The same person would probably have lauded the Olympics for its general 'brotherly', 'intercultural' and 'international' characteristics… claiming themselves to be 'tolerant', 'cosmopolitan', 'global', 'open-minded'…

240

Throughout my participation in international conferences, I have had quite different sentiments about how interculturality was unfolding as I was communicating with people from Africa, Asia and Latin America. There are a lot of dimensions exclusive to these types of intercultural encounters.

239

Mainstream interculturality is mostly concerned with types of intercultural encounters that are not political or controversial such as *international students*. It is not common to witness debates around religion, whiteness and racial capitalism, probably because these topics are unnecessarily ideological and pessimistic.

[*The political, economic and ideological as elements removed from view in research on interculturality*. However, pushing them aside leads to negating the very essence of interculturality (Dervin & Simpson, 2021; Ibelema, 2021; Atay et al., 2023; Dervin, 2022).]

238

Are Northern scholars required to move somewhere else to signal internationalization? They do not have to. They are indeed invited by others to be used as a symbol of internationalization although the underlying intent is to have them push their universities further and get a higher ranking.

[Seeing Northern scholars being invited to speak/preach ('spreach') about interculturality (alongside democracy, citizenship, intercultural competence) in the South often triggers a sense of schizophrenia in us.]

[Decolonial neurosis]

237

A colleague tells me that she was told to "use decoloniality in [your] paper because it is very popular at the moment and it will help you get your papers accepted in international journals if you speak the right *linguo*". *Maddening calculated nonsense.*

236

Decolonial and postcolonial theories have created this illusion in our psyches and minds that discourses and rhetorics would suffice; their theoretical arrangements deliver a mesmerizing epistemological complexity which has developed the fantasy that abstractism and theory are 'so good' that praxis is not always necessary. They have constructed a false bubble in which our voices and words are enough and which the Western cognitive empire has gladly welcomed.

235

Decoloniality is not a cliché yet as long as the reasonings for its existence are still adamant. Due to power asymmetries, the intercultural is decolonial and, therefore, the more decolonial, the more balanced and consequently the more intercultural. [At this moment, I am reconsidering whether decoloniality is still not a cliché *yet*; maybe it has always been but it is a space where some group's hardships make sense. Building on other's unfortunate social realities to advance our careers is an uncomfortable notion, but decoloniality could only move those who has felt being colonized in your thinking in the sense that one needs to tame what they think and say in order to respect those western conceptions of appropriateness, especially that if something is done in the US and UK, then it is the right thing. Even my people tell me this sometimes!]

234

In an attempt to decolonize the state of knowledge and perspective about creativities, responsiveness to diverse realities is necessary; discussing the need to involve alternative epistemologies and ontologies of creativity requires a sense of commensurability by taking into account the insights of critical scholars from the global south about their respective contexts, and this is what these two theories may offer. In the context of intercultural communication of creativities, they are two ways of going about the geopolitics of knowledge about aesthetics and the circulation of cultural productions and how they are understood as artistic, exotic or unoriginal rather than the postcolonial or decolonial frameworks per se.

233

I was invited to be a guest speaker. The theme was "social justice and decoloniality in education". The other speaker was a white person who has worked in several places in the Global South(s). I did not get to express myself because the other speaker took most of the time and interrupted me to drone on their travels (denoting how their passports are powerful that they can jump on planes without the hassle of a visa), telling the Global South(s) to use their own knowledges in their curricula (blaming the subaltern for their own subalternity). A white privileged person telling the Global South(s) how to exercise social justice and to decolonize; the tone was patronizing. I was not allowed to

Figure 2.1 (Stereotypical) representation of a 'foreign' figure at a Chinese museum

discuss the questions and remarks I had because the other speaker might have thought their discourses were more legitimate than mine. I told them: "what you are doing now is coloniality while we are discussing decoloniality". They got upset and left while I was talking! (Figure 2.1 shows the (stereotypical) representation of a 'foreign' figure at a Chinese museum. This figure urges us to reverse our take on who has the power to represent who *interculturally* and to reconsider the possibility of rebalancing the right to speak and to imagine).

232

Since creative practices are shaped by wider socio-historical contexts, specifically the situated experiences, beliefs and values (Hocking, 2018), postcoloniality has the possibility of not only offering critical understandings of past colonial relations but also of current systems of power which continue to influence the intercultural communication of creativities. Advancing a postcolonial frame of mind that recognizes decolonial knowledges and crea-tivities as a counter-hegemonic framework is an important step in reimagining the enduring influence of coloniality under the guise of modernity on global relations. To place artists from non-Western countries on an egalitarian basis, new ways of being should ideally imagine the trajectories of artistic produc-tion and its communication on the basis of an intercultural reality which is mutually transformative, e.g., consuming the Contra-Flow of K-pop in Spain (Yoon et al., 2020). By encouraging such practices, contemporary art may serve a participating function in the "necessary processes of political resist-ance and counter-hegemony" (McCarthy & Dimitriadis, 2000: 59).

231

I tend to critique the west and the Global North, but a recent experience has opened my eyes a bit more to reality. There was a project that I was leading with people from my society. I was highly motivated and keen on producing something of high quality that I contribute to my people. I concentrated on visibilizing their perspectives on language, culture and identity. However, as the project started moving forward, I started to notice a lack of commitment and work ethics. People assumed that simply because I speak for the peripher-ies, I would bypass whatever comes from the peripheries. They simply de-cided to rely on me to get the work done since I had exhibited enthusiasm and willingness to make effort. This act of conflating the personal and the professional is disturbing. Again, this is only related to a specific instance and with a few people, but I was asking myself whether these asymmetries and hierarchies between us and them are always the outcomes of the others' self-ascribed sense of superiority and their subordination of our communities. I sort of concluded that it is not the case, and my people are partially responsi-ble for their misfortunes as well. I cannot pretend that the west is the only side to blame. Decolonizing should presuppose honesty with oneself before ad-dressing others. Decolonization would not fix the lack of work ethics. Clutch-ing to decolonial discourses is only shifting the focus from some individuals' carelessness to others' historical structures and systems. We should not use magnifying glasses only when addressing others but also ourselves. The issue is again as soon as I would say something, I would be accused of standing on a pedestal preaching and sermonizing. I do not mind that as long as I do not lie to myself by blaming others for everything demanding that the world has to change without thinking of changing oneself first.

230

Decoloniality can realize the underlying premises of interculturality because it is not clear what interculturality we are referring to when reciprocality is not there.

[Should decoloniality precede interculturality or the other way around? Reciprocity is not necessary in interculturality since the *inter* could be fiction. *The fiction of interculturality* sounds like a great book title.]

[Inter as a fiction is indeed an interesting aspect to explore. When I speak of interculturality as reciprocity, somehow, I know that it is an illusion. Reciprocity requires honesty, modesty, equality, understanding, generosity (amongst others). In our capitalistic worlds, are these even possible since any relation has to rely on some form of give-and-take. Reciprocating would mean treating and be(coming) with others beyond power relations. An impossibility.]

229

It sometimes crosses my mind that the Global South could be also blamed for its subalternity. Decolonial discourses are not receiving interested ears and eyes who are at least willing to consider what these scholars have to offer. For them, anything that does not reflect immediate and/or visible impact is not needed. People seem to be okay with the fact that they are followers and colonized as long as they have some perks of those in the West.

228

Although my scholarships critique power asymmetries, I often do not afford to go against the waves and act as decolonial as I am supposed to. This discrepancy is very telling of how academia could be a hard place to navigate because one is torn between exercising decoloniality despite its consequences and pursuing one's goals and dreams.

227

A lot of decolonial accounts ask for citing southern scholars more – which is an argument that I support. However, citing Southern scholars should not be for the sake of citing them *per se* but for the importance of their works in understanding and making sense of the topic under investigation. Also, Southern scholars' perspectives may have more legitimacy over those of others on some issues, themes and topics. For instance, one cannot expect a work that discusses decoloniality without any reference to Southern scholars. But we should not aim for citing these scholars and use their works as ornaments to exemplify how we root for epistemic justice. This logic does not really contribute to epistemic justice because it remains a surface-level situation that does not address the core issues and the underlying causes. The main point here is to while citing is essential, what is more, important is drawing on their philosophies and understandings in our works; this practice would help visibilize their knowledges more effectively.

226

PhD students from the Global South who are pursuing their studies in the Global North need to aim at transcending their own supervisors. In decolonial logics, mental barriers and over-idealization of the other are killing oneself. They may be great but one has to seek to be greater. *Being someone's student is not an end in itself.*

225

It is important to recognize that the intercultural is decentring/decolonial and, thus, the more decentred/decolonized, the more intercultural and balanced it is. Analysing through the lenses of the post-colonial and decolonial theories grants a less American-Eurocentric understanding of the sophisticated layering of stratified systems; this would also supplement the theoretical frameworks that have been used in educational research to explain the colonial legacy in education. Yet, this attempt at Africanizing intercultural education should not lead to methodological nationalism/continentalism that may undo the possibility of conceiving knowledge, curriculum, pedagogy, theory and methodology as geopolitical constructs and tools constitutive of existing imperial/colonial relations within and between nation-states (Fúnez-Flores, 2021).

224

Decolonization is not an event that could take place over the course of a specific timeline. It is a long-term process that starts with delinking and ends with emancipation.

223

Decoloniality is often misunderstood; it is sometimes conceived to denote violence, aggression and coup.

222

Relationality is important in the postmodern world, but that should not transpire in the form of colonial relations among the states. That is why decoloniality is not about cutting ties with the Western colonial world but establishing reciprocality and balance in giving, taking and impacting.

221

Intercultural education is often thrown randomly whenever it fits the narrative without seriously engaging with its premises. The intercultural is decolonial and thus the more decolonial and decentring, the more intercultural it is.

220

This 'faction' of critical and decolonial scholars in interculturality research needs to exercise more solidarity by cross-citation and visibilizing/drawing on each other's works.

219

While we devote a substantial amount of energy to promoting decoloniality, our own people may simply prefer to cite Northern scholars.
[The vicious circle of rankings and citations, reproducing (neo-)colonial ties.]

218

It would be interesting to examine the geopolitical positionings of editors who superintend the works on decolonization, especially special issues editors. It is frightening how, despite the remarkable work on skewed geopolitics of knowledge, it is still the case that White northern scholars are in charge of administrating and flirting with the types of voices and narratives that get to theorize and discuss decolonization.

217

Some Northern scholarships may purport that they understand southern struggles but they may opt to discuss what is most relevant to their experiences. Sympathy does not mean genuine understanding and support. Sympathy can be patronizing and its manifestations may include tokenistic inclusion of the Global South to showcase the validity of the banners and slogans around 'decolonization' and 'diversity'.

216

We seem certain that the Global South wants to decolonize but it may be our 'ego' speaking – not the periphery.

215

Decolonization is about decolonizing systems, not just a few people.

214

We need to emphasize that, if interculturality is about making a difference and undermining inequalities, then the subaltern spaces need to be supported in making use of its epistemological and activist affordances within education to decolonize and decentre their learning spaces.

213

When everybody attempts to (or pretends to) decolonize everything then we run the risk that nothing is decolonizable by the end of the day.

212

There is a culture of subordination in the Global South. People simply do not mind being inferior and colonized. If it has been working for a while, then why risk it all? On the other hand, there have been some comments that blame the colonized nations for their colonization and that they were not civilized enough to protect their own spaces [or maybe some individuals feel, despite being colonized, that this is the best possible version of the world. Maybe, decolonization for them would mean deteriorating; coloniality of knowledge has been so domineering that it cripples the possibility of thinking of an alternative].

211

Western traditions seem to present themselves as caps for civilization. The subalterns have learned that western ontologies are not to be transcended but to be sought. Decolonization is not about the caps but rather about dismantling the whole underlying imaginations of caps. Decolonization is about transcending and imagining alternative ontologies. Decolonization is not about being non-western but indeed about not seeking to be western or non-western, simply seeking to be something that is not imposed on them. Decolonization is not emancipation but nullifying the need to emancipate.

210

White supremacy is a fundamental premise in coloniality and interculturality needs to inform its theories with these profound insights that broach serious and uncomfortable discussions. [It is more yielding to focus on non-whiteness as it would construct various levels of analysis; it is essential to understand the reverberations of coloniality in our minds to disrupt them. Being uncolonizable is more probably more important than being decolonizable; the latter is a painful process.]

[Research and interculturality: disconnection from reality]

209

Research on interculturality is crowd-consumed but it is not as crowded as it should be.

208

Scholars from the Global South are seen as great data collectors. If one wants to research 'Africa', they have to include a co-author from that space as a way of safeguarding one's immunity from critique under the premise that one is taking what does not belong to them. Some scholars from the Global South would not probably mind as long as they get to publish.

[I am thinking of many examples of scholars from Mainland China who have collected 'sensitive' data about 'minorities' for Western scholars. They get included in publications, endorse their contents by being placed as 'co-author' and yet they are often unaware of the patronizing and misleading (a-contextualized and westernized) interpretations of the data that they have provided. Although their institutions benefit from their inclusion in top journals, should they read the content of their publications, they might not feel so proud of their achievements.]

207

A substantial amount of research in interculturality deflects attention from the very concerns and issues framing intercultural relations; the overfocus on benevolent and innocuous topics such as identity, self and others belies the main structures that have shaped interculturality throughout history.

206

There is a staggering amount of miseducation taking place around critical issues and other people's struggles. There is a tendency to overload mainstream perspectives and knowledges with epistemic nationalism in the sense that little effort is paid to understand others through their own lenses. Especially in interculturality, it is difficult to simply take the freedom to start theorizing on behalf of others in ways that are not even accessible to them. If intercultural scholars are eager to expand their horizons by researching others, specifically in the Global South, one has to be willing to undergo some deep epistemic changes and transformations that accompany the process of exploring others. One cannot be epistemologically rigid in interculturality since some ontologies do defy our normative understandings of humans and their actions and philosophies.

205

Reading a new call for conference papers about interculturality I am reminded of the 'whateverism' of intercultural research and education. *Anything goes. No meaning. No controversy.* Just a list of topics – or should I say *ideological entries*! In that sense, this call corresponds well to some of the realities of interculturality.

204

By using *http://opensyllabus.org/* and looking for the keyword 'intercultural', I was not surprised that the most frequently assigned title is Samovar's (1972) "Intercultural Communication: A Reader" which is a typical text that heavily draws on essentialist representations and moralistic judgments of others' ontologies, knowledges and perspectives that reify cultural differences and thus, create systems of privilege/subordination. It is astonishing how recent critical research may not be featured on the syllabus despite the recurrent critique of such knowledges. Interculturality may be emptied of its geopolitical implications by adamantly clutching to the old essentialist perspectives that refuse to refrain from classifying people and delineating boundaries among cultures. This type of findings broaches again the question of whether education is keeping abreast of the epistemological developments in research. Once intercultural education research is integrated without taming and attenuating its ideological and controversial claims, then we can discuss the type of impact our discourses have on real life.

203

The amount of discussion and recommendations in education research is over whelming to teachers. In many countries, teachers are not paid much, which is incommensurate with the type of tasks and missions that are assigned. For instance, knowing how much teachers get in Morocco, it is indeed domineering and morally embarrassing to ask teachers to read the most recent scholarships and to make extra efforts to implement scholars' ideas. We have to admit that we often place ourselves in an ivory tower without any attempt to approach teachers' struggles and we readily assume that they have the right and convenient set of circumstances to apply what we preach. Sometimes, we may even think that they are consciously refusing to take our insights into consideration without really considering their contextual factors. Teachers in Morocco, for instance, are incredibly overwhelmed by the schools' conditions, class size, students' level as well as students' and parents' conservatism in terms of opening up to the novel, creative and innovative approaches. It feels far-fetched to ask these teachers to read and materialize our idealistic and complex perspectives and methodologies.

202

The only future for interculturality in research and education lies in mythologizing its mythologies.

201

The chameleon in intercultural research changes concepts, ideas, methods and even political beliefs following trends. They do not invent or look for inspiration from afar but just borrow and, like a weather wane, turns with the wind. Interculturality is just an instrument for the chameleon. The chameleon does not propose anything, but they just adopt 'things' for their own benefits and turn to other 'things' when the wind changes directions.

200

It is constantly on my mind how Darwin relied on nature to explain the superiority of certain races. Even the most outstanding thinkers and philosophers were the most vocal racists and supremacists. Heidegger, Kant, Hegel and Hobbs are some of the unapologetic scholars that assign grotesque inherent superiority to their races and disparage others' humanity. It is absolutely necessary that we consider how similar understandings may be rationalized and popularized in contemporary research through subtle analytical theories and masked conclusions. One does not have to marginalize others openly, they simply have to silently, but through action, reaffirm the intellectual superiority and fineness of themselves and their people.

199

It is indeed important to ascertain that published knowledge is scientific, rigorous and original. However, these parameters can be subjective and applied quite differently to assess the merits and legitimacies of a particular study. What is more critical is the way these parameters can be employed to discredit research that we do not understand or does not conform to our understandings of epistemology and research.

[“I don't see Byram et al. being included in the book. Any serious work on interculturality must cite them”, a reviewer told me recently. *Opinion versus contribution to knowledge?*]

198

Citations are certainly one of the main ways of measuring “impact”. Correlating numbers with how much power someone's work has had, and how much it shapes colleagues' work. Fogarty (2009) argues that citations have become the currency of academia. Yet, what is often ignored is how our citing practices may reflect and re-enact epistemological injustices (Ennser-Kananen, 2019).

We need to question our citation 'routines' and ask ourselves whether we cite works based on their rigour and contribution or based on the reputation and the fame of the authors. I can venture to argue that early careers may not feel 'free' to manage their citations in whatever ways they are convinced by. What I mean is that they cite some people just for the sake of pleasing editors and reviewers. Established scholars may not particularly concern themselves with these practices since they have the power to convince others of the legitimacy of what they say and the types of works they choose to draw on.

197

Citations should be used as an 'insight' into the intellectual and epistemological contribution of scholars. These numbers are 'murdering' the very essence of what science is about. Widely cited "scholars" do not mean the most rigorous and/or the most brilliant. Disciplines are different and some lines of thought are more citable than others. For instance, in language education, works get cited numerous times since it is a popular field where books and articles are published on daily basis leading to a massive number of publications every year. In interculturality, things are a bit different where although a lot of works are published, they are not as citable as other fields. One can compare the number of academic journals specializing in language education and interculturality to be able to recognize the difference. Again, these dimensions should be taken into account and readers need to understand that citations are framed by geopolitical considerations including the author's affiliation, the context of research, the language used and the *cite-me-I-cite-you* policy. I am not convinced by citations and I hope others would express their dissatisfaction with this numeric criterion in academia.

[Silencing or usurping voices by not citing them (properly) are not unknown phenomena in intercultural research.]

196

Those who are not widely cited cannot be perceived to have less rigorous work and, therefore, cannot have any influence on the fields and colleagues' perspectives. Influence is not defined by one's epistemic contributions but defined by the geopolitical parameters that decide who gets to be influential.

195

The peer-review process may sometimes require authors to read and cite certain references. It is often not deliberate, by authors, not to draw on these works.

Some scholars do not have access to the most recent literature and the only literature available to them is open-access articles and books. We cannot simply assume that everyone enjoys the same privilege since some people do their best based on the resources offered to them.

194

Taking part in a project involving Morocco, China and Finland was remarkably insightful. The very experience of seeing smiles and nice words exchanged among each other without prejudice and/or pre-conceived thoughts exemplifies the type of interculturality I envisage to permeate the imbalanced world. The most important dimension was how students were eager to learn about each other. This instance has given me hope that interculturality research could make a difference in some people's perceptions of others. Moving forward, we need to contextualize our perspectives and involve people more in ways that do not disconnect our scholarships from their lived experiences.

193

The 'hidden' transcendental power of numbers and figures in intercultural research.

192

There are misplacements that cannot be accepted in research. I see for instance an amalgam of references between brackets to justify a somewhat banal idea in a journal article on interculturality (reference to a young scholar followed by a reference to Claude Lévi-Strauss) – the idea of *bricolage*, a somewhat funny looking and sounding French word from a verb for *to fiddle, tinker*. This resembles aggrandizing while illustrating well *bricolage* at its worst.

191

Theory, ontology, epistemology. These are all Greek words. These all give us orders from a specific corner of the world. These tell us what we can and should do in research. These might all need trashing.

190

With all the *re-imagining* going on in research on interculturality today, soon, we will all be hired by Disney. Is there really anything to *re-imagine* today? Is it about re-imagining or re-ideologizing?

189

The other is often considered as a ghost to 'bust' in intercultural research and education.

188

Too many fetishes in intercultural research and education.

187

Too much demophobia (Crépon, 2012) in the way interculturality is used in research and education. We don't listen to people, we ask them to listen to us! This disregard will lead to no one listening to researchers and educators one day.

186

Research is obviously too spectralon-like – this whitest material ever produced in the universe which reflects over 99% of the light hitting it. Many other colours in education and research also act as if they were *spectralonesque*.

185

Most research on interculturality today sounds like mere echoes.

184

The Emma Bovary Syndrome of research on interculturality (e.g. about Hofstede and Deardorff): I have not read these scholars but I condemn them. Those who censored Flaubert's novel, *Madame Bovary* published in 1857, hardly ever read it before making the decision to remove it from bookstore shelves. The same is probably true of 'classics' of interculturality who are condemned today without being read. I remember a colleague who often criticized Huntington and his clash of civilizations but who confessed that he had never read the book…

183

Many dominating ideologies in the field of interculturality have become 'traditions' today. We should not abandon ourselves to such 'traditions' but consider them critically. Like traditions, they need to change with time and space.

In old French, *a tradition* was a statement, belief or practice handed down from generation to generation. Reading through today's research I see many mere such statements, beliefs and practices.

182

My scholarships are most relevant to those subaltern people in the peripheries; however, most of them cannot afford to access my work. I often receive requests to share some papers which I gladly favourably reply to, but what about the others? They end up making use of knowledges available online upon their first Google search. Also, they cannot keep abreast of the latest research because their universities cannot afford to subscribe. The issue is not only knowledge production but also knowledge consumption.

181

Reading research papers on interculturality I feel that we scholars have hijacked, kidnapped the notion. Standing above all, we determine what it is and what it does. We have become its creator. However, it is interculturality that generates us…

180

Feeling of *fake big sky* (a Chinese idiom) in reading about what interculturalists predict should be researched in the future. *Same agendas. Same emptiness. Same keywords. Same tribes. Same doxa.*

179

Everything is open to re-interpretation, re-appraisal and re-structuring including those historical 'facts' or the theories of our admired research idols.

178

Academia can cause a lot of distress to those who are trying to survive. Keeping up with the metrics, expectations and comparisons can be overwhelming and ultimately undo the very essence of research and science.

177

We cannot be interculturally selective: doing research and establishing collaborations only when it is convenient.

[Words write us]

176

"Don't just use one sentence paragraph", writes a reviewer for one of my papers.

[Let's use a popular 'concept': *Micro-aggression.*]

175

I ask colleagues who write about interculturality who it is that they write for. *Silence.* They don't know. They have never thought about it. They write – that's all. Writing is intercultural *par excellence.* Ghosting them is going against the notion.

[A colleague calls my recent books 'textbooks'. After enquiring why, they note that I ask questions to my readers... Including you readers could mean this book is 'downgraded' to the category of a 'mere' textbook.]

174

Isn't it interesting that we humans can write about a phenomenon that cannot but resonate with us as persons and yet ignore its principles in the ways we write about it?

173

Readers could be hell for the writers. Readers do not often sympathize because they tend to read only what they want.

172

I am writing about interculturality but I am certainly not the most intercultural individual.

171

Hart (2011) presented a biologically based explanation as a rationale for the use of an 'epistemic positioning strategy' by speakers/writers so as to assign more legitimacy to theories and assertions with the ultimate aim of persuading consumers of their knowledge of the rigour and soundness of their perspectives.

170

Colonia in Latin (which obviously gave the word *colony* in English) contains *-cola,* the idea of the *inhabitant.* Interestingly this cannot but remind us of a famous American drink… [The red drink of 'happiness' in China. The drink of global dominance in some parts of the world.]

169

The 'Chinese' idea of 'cultural dissemination' (an idea found in many other contexts, often behind other words and phrases) could easily be a synonym for '(inter)cultural propaganda'.

168

Forced, tailored and structured academic language conceals a lot of implicit prejudices. We often do not use the right words to describe the atrocities of certain phenomena because we have to 'balance' and 'tone down'.

167

Lingua-politics produces words imposed on scholars by decision-makers. Linguapolitics is often broad, polysemous in nature so as to attract as many people as possible and make them rehearse and spread these words to the masses. No one really knows what they are talking about. Nevermind: As long as one gets funding, publications and a little bit of fame.

166

Floating past each other at a PhD defence in France. I listen to colleagues talking about interculturality but I have this impression of solitary discourses and positionings. In other words, I do not understand what they are talking about. I can make sense of the words that they use one by one but pieced together they sound like rehearsed slogans. Am I solitary in my own thinking?

165

Seen in an interculturalist's biodata in Chinese. *Prof. xxx has many disciples whom she has trained over the years* (i.e. students). Is it a coincidence that the word *disciples* shares the same roots as *discipline* – a Proto-Indo European root referring to *take* and *accept*? I have never considered either *taking* or *accepting* as what summarizes my relations to my 'students'. *Co-taking, yes. Refusing instead of accepting.*

164

The polyglot (a big strong word) is a linguistic nomad, according to Braidotti (1994). *Fair enough.* However, although a nomad moves, they always go back to the same places. Knowing many languages does not necessarily mean opening up one's worlds...

163

A PhD researcher insists on using the somewhat misleading and polysemous term of *moral education* in English to refer to deyu (德育) education in China – a term that encompasses citizenship, politics, well-being, ideology... When I see the word 'moral education' I know that people from different corners of the world will imagine different things when engaging with it.

162

"It is becoming increasingly clear that we cannot overcome our underdevelopment and dependence unless we try to understand the imperialist character of Western social science and to exorcise the attitudes of mind which it indicates" (Ake, 1979: II); this quote can be a reminder of how for those who have gone through the hardships of colonialism and coloniality, it is challenging to discuss certain matters using diplomatic and soft language. Real-life experiences are reverberated into words and reading the literature for example allows people to fully grasp the atrocity of particular events and how they have had a lasting impact on people's psyches and minds.

161

Why is it that the question *'in what language do you dream?'* is asked almost systematically to a so-called polyglot? That's in fact a very strange question to ask to 'understand' this character. In the 'mess' of dreams, where one loses one's sense of realities, how could one know the languages one uses? In dreams, a so-called monolingual can be plurilingual and, even, omnilingual (use any language) – a *somnilingual* in a sense... someone who can dream in any language. The very question 'in what language'... (note the singular) is a way to try to rationalize the other, to pretend that one can make sense of who they are, to lock them up in categories, with the aim to 'nationalize' them ('one language' usually means 'one nation'). The question is bad investment. No answer close enough to the realities will get us to the polyglot's complexities.

160

I see the phrase 'heritage language maintenance' again and I cannot help picturing a car being repaired. Would we accept to use such a mechanistic term to refer to privileged individuals – whose language does not really need to be 'maintained'? [Their heritage is safe and sound, so it is a-heritage].

159

Some of us impose their language(s) onto us to speak about interculturality while others just use these languages because they have no choice. What and how they then speak about is not really *theirs*.

158

In Morocco, speaking French makes one sound educated while speaking English makes one sound educated, liberal and cool. It is astonishing how each language indexes different ontologies. This is not exclusive to the Global South, but also in places like Finland (as in the case of the Swedish language).

157

The polyglot is perceived as an irrational being whom we try to rationalize – reduce to one language amongst many languages.

156

Interculturality without the Global South is nothing; it revolves around itself without genuine considerations of what interculturality actually 'is'. [I tend to use the Global South as a concept in most of my discourses; this may have been critiqued on the basis of its reinforcement of binaries; I am asking whether this matters, and how it could help disrupt inequalities. I leave this for readers to reflect on; I want to remind them that I use the Global South as an adjective rather than a notion that delineates certain places to be peripheral or not.]

155

I am not sure what some concepts mean although I have used them many times. Concepts are there to be used not to be understood, I surmise.

154

Some theorizations and discussions of interculturality in language education that prioritize simplicity and accessibility may be undermining and impinging on the epistemological complexities of intercultural relations.

[The 'critical': a new opium]

153

"Encourage students to be critical thinkers!". And yet don't bother to be critical (of your own criticality) yourself!

152

Criticality fatigue at the moment. Critical as a mere slogan.

151

It is not clear whether these critical scholarships in interculturality are meaningful since the people who need them the most completely ignore their insights, perceptions and praxis as they adamantly continue to draw on dominant knowledges and discourses.

150

We keep discussing how the Global North has recently maintained its dominance and power, but we tend to overlook how the Global South(s) would have been doing the same if there had had the same resources. Coloniality and control are not products of the west, but rather products of humanity. Who is powerful would like to preserve their authority at the expense of the other because they are aware that the other would do the same if things were to overlap.

149

Two scholars pretending to be doing criticality of criticality describe their identities by mentioning their skin colour (white), their sexual orientation (straight) and age (middle-/old). How about declaring their (active) connections with the 'real' Global South (beyond 'tokens'), political affiliations, how much money is available on their bank accounts, their properties, their darkest thoughts, etc.? Declaring a couple of selected ('easy') identities can too easily de-responsibilize.

148

Criticality has now even become an opportunity for pretending and giving 'intercultural' lessons to others. The misused idea of 'locus of enunciation' appears to be a good tool to do so.

147

Heard a presentation by a PhD student from the Middle East today about interculturality in English textbooks. *Full of Western-centrisms! Full of Western gurus!* The student uses *their voices* to *announce* that textbooks in the Middle East are full of stereotypes about the Brits… She also adds, through *their voices* again, that students in the Middle East are not good critical thinkers… Get rid of these voices!

146

Education is a relatively more interesting field of inquiry since it is open to critical theories and frameworks. Applied Linguistics still seems to clutch its inherent understandings and knowledges.

145

'Critical' ideas such as *liquid interculturality, 'small' cultures* and *transculturing self* are still very much Eurocentric. Labelling them as 'critical' does not really make any difference in front of the epistemic injustice of the field. They still serve the same privileged figures.

144

Artworks are not always regular, meaning that they may not be always lucid in terms of their significance and substance. Theorizing art might not be sufficiently constructive except "through a semiotic/representationalist paradigm that limits what we can do, beyond trying often fruitlessly and usually contentiously to interpret the content" (DeMarrais & Robb, 2013: 4). These narratives or interpretations are, thus, expected to be formed by the possession of profound knowledge of all the interrelating layers. This knowledge is indispensable for comprehending/interpreting creativities and artworks as embedded in cultural infrastructures. Since artworks rarely exist in a vacuum as they are often anchored in a particular ontology (artistic, social, cultural…), communicating creativities should be grounded in critical perspectives about historical, cultural and political realities that discursively define an artistic production. It is important to engage with the communication of creativities by examining intersecting social categorizations and overlapping systems of marginalization/privilege that constitute power relations among groups, especially cross-culturally. Intercultural communication of any ideas, knowledge and objects is not always mutually fulfilling given the imbalances in South-West cultural exchanges due to hegemonic effects; therefore, communication of creativities may reflect these contradictions, imbalances and inequities.

143

Enough with perspectives on interculturality pretending to be 'critical' while looking to defend the *status quo*!

142

In forgetting to look at themselves in the mirror, a lot of critical perspectives on interculturality – targeted at others – are mere caricatures of themselves.

141

As I am currently working on a study examining Moroccan university students' acculturation dynamics towards Sub-Saharan students, I feel that the same over-lapping systems of privilege/subordination between the Global North and South are exercised again, but this time among the Global South(s) and within them. I am Moroccan and I know, beyond what the study shows, that some individuals may have a superior perception of themselves over people coming from other African countries. The implicit assumption underpinning this imagination is that while Morocco could be within the peripheries, other African countries are even more subaltern. Some spaces are more Southern than others, and that showcases how power asymmetries are reflected through and within various levels bringing about a myriad of dynamics situating people in different boxes depending on their geopolitical location within a particular realm, field and context. The con-cern is that we recycle what we critique and re-project it against others.

140

Intercultural philosophy is an interesting subfield of interculturality. It makes some interesting remarks about the notion. However, the critiques it addresses are still revolving around overly western voices as if *the other* could not talk.

139

Acculturation is such an interesting approach. It is rarely critiqued on the basis of its essentialist underpinnings because it presents the process of relinquish-ing one's cultural specificities and embracing others as a straightforward pro-cess [acculturation sounds like snakes shedding their skin].

[Miscellaneous critiques]

138

As ideologues, we all contribute to both impoverish and annihilate the notion of interculturality.

137

Face-to-face encounters are not the only forms of interculturality. *This schizo-phrenic belief is very much resistant!* Interculturality is occurring everywhere, every minute of our lives, within and between us.

136

A very powerful memory from a French actress whose father used to ask her not to look at herself in the mirror. He would say: "Get out of the mirror, you are going to dirty it". This is what most of us tell those willing to learn from others about their own ways of discoursing about interculturality.

135

The cliché of the world as a *global village. No, the world is not global.* We are very much divided linguistically, epistemologically, politically, financially, technologically ('Chinese' social media vs. 'Western' social media), etc. *Let's stop lying to ourselves!*

134

A conference call entitled *Intercultural communication: Synergies in languages, professions and heritages.* I read the call several times. *I hear the soft wind.*

133

"I studied abroad to meet people who are different". In times of environmental emergencies like today, let's save our pennies to stay home. Difference flourishes *here* too.

132

Ideology is also a windscreen for interculturality.

131

To distract is to create an alternative reality where one's misfortunes are denied, masked and misrepresented.

130

Distracting some people is a vocal manifestation that these people are distractable and they probably mean little to those who distract.

129

Politics of distraction could also be a benevolent act in the sense that those who distract wish not to blame or showcase the accountability of people for their misfortunes.

128

Politics of distraction are an impressive mechanism of manipulation. They could also illuminate how research tends to emphasize apolitical stances that solve little but supplied misleading interpretations of reality. [I am wondering to what extent we are distracting as well; it is probably a never-ending process of distracting and being distracted. Distraction may be necessary to bear the crudeness of our lives and experiences. I imagine how life may be more difficult of we were all brutally honest.]

127

Moroccan officials would argue that Moroccan public schools and universities are doing well when they would do everything in their power to educate their children in French and English private schools and send them later to France, Canada or US. Those who are financially comfortable would always prefer having their children educated abroad, while those who can't, would trust the public universities to educate their kids and ultimately obtain a degree that would get them a stable job. Financial disparities among Moroccans are stark that the public discourses seem like completely inattentive to the people's struggles.

126

For Kristeva (1984), between *the object* and *the subject*, there is *the abject* – the crisis of identity *par excellence*. Discourses of citizenship and democracy in relation to interculturality today push us to imagine the abject of the notion, disregarding both object and subject.

125

It is not wise to apply the same criteria to judge two people: conditions, circumstances and opportunities are often the main things that determined one's trajectory.

124

Someone sharing an ad for a speaker within the field of interculturality in China adds the following comment: "The Goddess is coming!". Worship kills intercultural scholarship. 'Engodding' scholars kills our thinking.

123

Reading through announcements for talks I cannot help thinking about videos of people showing off their muscles online but who don't show their faces. Long biodatas with all kinds of 'achievements' and yet nothing about their ideas and contributions. *Muscles before brains…*

122

Untrusted epistemologies are defined by their geopolitical location rather than their epistemic capacities.

121

I am feeling uneasy about how some notions are sacred. I am not sure how epistemologically sound is the implicit assumption that particular notions have to be used and seen in certain discussions. This practice limits our imaginative and subjective understanding of social reality.

120

Doing interculturality in academia might not be easier than in real life.

119

Privilege could, in some cases, explain why some people are 'brilliant' or 'not'.

118

People are as intercultural as only society allows them to be.

117

Sometimes, the only difference between people of god and thieves is circumstances and conditions, not the will. People of god could have easily been the thieves if they had lived in the conditions of the thieves. [No one makes decisions by absolute freedom. No one is free. One may say that I get to choose what I like, but unfortunately no one chooses what they 'like'. Should I be blamed if I was a thief when the only possibility seems to be so? Should I be praised that I am a man of god when I get to clutch to the very idea that my principles are way more sublime than others?]

116

The white symbolizes modernity and prosperity for a lot of individuals and societies. One reason for this assumption is the privileged's unwillingness to endanger their position by being associated with or seen in and among the subaltern.

115

Reading the other could be an oppressive act whereby we apply our situated intellectual frameworks and through which we assign a particular 'assessment' of the other. We may be reading the other in contexts, situations and moods that do not do justice to the works we are perusing.

114

Wittgenstein's beetle in a box metaphor is relevant for reconsidering the way we discourse interculturality in research and education. For Wittgenstein (2009), we are all beetles in our boxes; we can hear each other's 'noises' but we cannot feel each other, we cannot sympathize necessarily (genuinely) with each other.

113

Knowledge is not notions and the notions should not be as ends in themselves but rather rigorous or, in some cases, inaccurate descriptions of social realities [what I mean here is that sometimes social realities are twisted to fit the notions not the other way around].

112

A Chinese colleague wants to work on what they call 'cultural emotions'. They explain that these have to do with both building up one's own confidence and love for one's 'culture'. When I ask them what 'culture' referred to, they reply that they don't know. When I note that I have seen the phrase 'cultural emotions' misused by many Chinese leaders (and scholars) in Chinese and English, they agree and maintain that they have no choice but follow dominating ideologies in China. I tell them that we all follow such ideological orders – *everywhere around the world.*

111

Culture is not something out there separated from society, politics, etc. It is part and parcel of all of them!

110

Those who cannot be easily extracted from may be excluded and pushed to the margins.

109

So-called theories of interculturality cannot but be mere *Weltanschauung* ('worldview') – they close the door to other standpoints.

108

It is possible to continue advancing the narrative that the Global South needs to be recognized but it is also essential to remind the peripheral contexts that disrupting the colonial mindset of Southern subjects is as indispensable as inviting the Global North to allow some space for alternative epistemologies.

107

Based on my autoethnographic narratives, for a lot of people in the peripheries, the Global North is the mirror through which they look at themselves. That is, their proximity to western ideals and ontologies as well as the validation they receive from the Global North are the standards against which one's ability, capacity and merit are assessed, perceived and understood.

106

The beauty of interculturality is that one can easily claim the relevance of any perspective or a topic to its scope. [As long as it is supported by those who have the power to speak in research and education.]

105

There is a lot of freedom in not being 'outstanding' or the 'odd one out'. [It may sound patronizing again but it may not sound so coming from some-one who is actually 'not outstanding'. Sometimes, what matters is who says what and then we build our understandings of what is being said on the who said that.]

104

A lot of students from Morocco would study abroad for the sole purpose of coming back and be assigned more epistemic credibility in terms of their qual-ifications, skills and expertise.

103

Pastiche of Agamben's (2004: 26) (about anthropology but fantasized for in-terculturality): "the device for producing the recognition of the human".

102

The construction of unequal knowledges started under colonialism and its continuities are perpetuated through structural power imbalances (de Sousa Santos, 2021; Mignolo, 2021). Colonial mindset, linguistic/epistemic de-pendency, racial discrimination and postcolonial malaise of Southern people further reenact and entangle their historical ineptitude as knowing subjects. The sociopolitical construction/maintenance of coloniality is an ongoing process that is continuously self-revamping and self-actualizing through harsh and uncompromising dynamics. Precipitating the invisibility of that colonial process is inextricably linked to the stability of subalternizing intri-cacies and epistemic inequities. Intercultural education is one of the fields that claim to emphasize the disruption of linguistic, cultural and epistemic hierarchies. Intercultural education is seemingly a philosophical compass for politicizing language, culture and epistemology; however, its founda-tional underpinnings are largely informed by western epistemologies and logics (R'boul, 2022a, b; 2023).

101

We can use numbers to make sense of intercultural reasonings and skills, but people are not numbers and realities are not models.

100

The myth of the *kitchen hen*. If you draw a circle around it, it won't step outside of it. By drawing similar circles around scholars and educators for interculturality, leaving them in their own ideological worlds, unfortunately, the myth survives.

99

Intercultural communication of arts can be a more complex business than intercultural communication of messages, meanings and ideas. Arts are within metaphysics and, thus, their delivery and reception are processed through different factors and conditions than those of intercultural communication. Arts are more intricate because their ontological state is never fixed or obvious.

98

I am not a big fan of numbers because they represent reality as capturable, fixed and countable.

97

Whoever says that one can be trained to act interculturally is running the risk of propagating a dangerous assumption that interculturality is simple to the extent that we can create systematic and organized plans to control intercultural relations.

96

Shining in academia stipulates moving to other countries. However, this movement entails a substantial emotional burden on us, Southern scholars. The closeness to family members and friends made me reconsider my decisions and whether moving abroad is worth it. At the moment of writing this line, I am having a bittersweet feeling. Leaving a comfort zone and seeking to ensure a brighter future in an actual instance of interculturality are motivating, but as scholars, we tend to downplay the personal and the emotional.

95

Interculturality is about sharing spaces, resources and power. When the distribution of wealth and power is imbalanced, the burden to ensure the functioning of intercultural encounters may be borne by the peripheries.

94

Interculturality cannot be achieved as long as colonial-like relations are ubiquitous and manifested in daily experience, language, knowledge and education.

93

Inequalities are adamant since they have fixated based on their historical continuities that have consolidated the very fundamental conditions that have created these injustices in the first place.

92

The use of the definite article *the* to speak of intercultural (amongst others) goes against the very principle of interculturality as a knotty and unseizable element.

91

Alternative knowledges of interculturality and intercultural education cannot be visibilized when they are seen and assessed through western lenses. The peripheries could be investing a lot of time and energy to end up having their works reviewed and appraised by the perspectives and epistemologies that they are trying to disrupt.

90

I always wonder whether people or systems are responsible for inequalities and power asymmetries. Although people create systems, they lead in their own ways once put in place; systems start to influence how people see the world especially when they are structured to overshadow some and visibilize others. Systems mould people in a sense and steer their sight to recognize some dimensions and not others. The systems may, for example, overemphasize how immigrants are taking the citizens' jobs and ignore how immigrants could be propelling the country's economy by doing those low-paid jobs; Yet again, some immigrants are highly skilled individuals with degrees and PhDs. For instance, after WW2, a lot of German scientists and scholars escaped the aftermath of the war by moving to the US. Those scientists brought substantial knowledge and expertise that the US still built on to move forward. It is more important to redress and amend systems than people.

89

Interculturality in education should not be a technology of power of the Western cognitive empire to normalize power asymmetries.

88

Coming from Africa, I feel that I am burdened with the task of ensuring the smooth functioning of intercultural encounters. I always have to attenuate any potentially culturally embedded practice or idea. The Global South(s) are incessantly interculturalizing but I am not sure that the Global North is returning the favour.

87

Too many documents from the UNESCO and COE show too much self-confidence about interculturality to be true. Interculturality must remain unsettled – *not reassuring.*

86

Politics is always there. Most will say 'power' without naming what it is really! P O L I T I C S. Why remove it? Why pretend it is not there? Isn't it because we interculturalists are in fact politicians?

85

On a 'global' (but in fact Western-centric) mailing list on interculturality, a US-based scholar wishes to stimulate a conversation around what matters for the members 'research-wise'. *Democracy-talk, environment-talk, banality-talk.* "What a great conversation! Let's keep it going". Someone from the Global South puts forward epistemic injustice in the field. *Silence. The conversation stops.* [Was there even a conversation?]

84

The peripheries cannot overcome their subalternity, underdevelopment and dependence unless they shatter adamant understandings of the benevolence of everything coming from the West. The peripheries have to attempt to understand in order to disrupt the imperialist character of humanities and social sciences.

83

It is surprising how my works get more recognition and visibility in the Global North than among my people although the main argument of my works is calling for more epistemic justice that includes the Global South as a fundamental enunciator and resource for theory and praxis.

82

It is a frightening conception that what you know and say is valued on the basis of your geopolitical location. [We cannot assume that we are untouched by the configurations of relations within knowledge; we all 'know' but the very fact "we know in different ways" is translated into "some know more than others".]

81

The very word interculturality has a European taste.

80

Academia might be a black hole where whatever gets inside is baptized into endorsing what is mainstream and dominant in order to advance in one's career.

79

All our theories and perspectives are bound by time, space and place. Some theories do not make sense to the peripheries and/or the Global North.

78

In academia, it is important to remain politically neutral to be respected, celebrated and invited as keynotes and assume leading positions. However, the politically neutral is not exciting and most of the important things that have to be said are not politically neutral.

77

A politically neutral approach is a clever tool to suppress those who go against the mainstream and to diminish the input on these issues around which debate and discussion can never be politically neutral.

76

We are all *doxosophers* of interculturality somehow. We all spread some kind of doxa about interculturality. Although nothing can be done about it, awareness and discussions around doxosophy allow us to change a little.

75

Interculturality may never fulfil its inherent premises.

74

It sometimes feels that interculturality is a daydream in which we discuss imaginary notions and practices that have nothing to do with realities.

73

I do understand how artistic expressions could be perceived through various forms of ontological processing depending on the type of socialization, knowledge and culture one has been nurtured within. There is a valid case for having artistic expressions made sense of simultaneously through similar and different trajectories. The epistemological fluidity of artistic expressions may not always emanate from the creative production per se but rather from how individuals establish varying understandings of that product by drawing on different resources of knowledge about that piece. While arts have a wide range of epistemologies constructed by the artist, they are detached from their individual experience to be open to re-interpretation, re-finding and re-processing because creative productions are to be navigated, subjectively sensed and felt rather than logically fathomed.

72

Arts are ontologies and ecologies of social reality but represented through situated imaginations that do not have to abide by any known principles. Yet, this state of fluidity creates a sense of difficulty in having the artist's perspective shared on grounds that could bear similar significance for the receiver. One could venture to claim that there is an inherent epistemological risk in artistic productions because one can hardly ascertain the delivery of their intended input.

[Fantasizing interculturality]

71

No matter how someone could be interculturally experienced, there is a high probability that they carry some essentialist perceptions of others. It is always easier to form a coherent and ready-made idea about the other without having to process differing signals and perspectives that pose a considerable amount of complexity.

70

I am not sure that I would ever be able to discuss the others quite comfortably if I present myself to be an expert of their ecologies, knowledges and ontologies. It is incredible how a lot of insights that are widely endorsed today are simply flawed and based on a short-sighted perspective of the world.

69

Southern people and scholars are recruited to adopt white western logics and behaviours that assign them some superiority over the societies they originally come from. For instance, a lot of Moroccans take pride in their education, work or simply residence in a country in the Global North. There are strata among degrees of pride depending on the privilege reverberations of these countries in Moroccans' psyches and minds. Studying or working in France is impressive but it is not comparable to studying or working in Canada. Nordic countries are specifically admired and used as ways to reinforce someone or something's high quality and attractiveness.

68

We tend to be epistemic approval junkies when we constantly seek endorsement from those we admire.

67

Interculturality can be a frustrating line of inquiry when its litanies are unshakeable in ways that idolize certain scholars and their theories.

66

The need to deconstruct stereotypes is a stereotype of today.

65

Interculturality in mainstream knowledges is fancy, unrealistic and idealistic.

64

We, scholars, take the freedom to speak on behalf of our societies, which again could be another act of intellectual superiority that the Global North exercises.

63

Interculturality is a very cloudy field since you can talk about almost anything and argue that it has some strong links to its rationales and concerns.

62

Interculturality allowed me to see inequalities more clearly. Interculturality opened my eyes to how the undertaker and mourner can be the same person.

61

The social and political construction of interculturality is a never-ending process. Invisibilizing the imbalances that condition intercultural relations is necessary to maintaining these hierarchies intact. Taking a neutral stance carries a great deal of culpability, especially from those whose status enables them to produce an immense effect.

60

The predominant sentiment is that essentialism in reifying cultural traits, differences and similarities is obsolete. However, we can argue that our understandings of some nations are fundamentally based on these essentialist assumptions. Although I join the criticisms of essentialism, I think they are useful in a sense because they carry some truth to it, at least around some individuals in some places.

59

Message from a colleague who has not been in touch for a very long time. Following a couple of 'polite salutations' (the tired 'I hope you are doing good') they ask for help to identify literature around 'Chinese intercultural communication'. *I reply that intercultural communication does not have any passport.*

58

Interculturality generated substantial insights that explain but may not do enough to make changes into reality. Discussing identity, self and other, and essentialism is apolitical and soft and entails little relevance to how the world is functioning. Intercultural encounters are unfair as much as the universe is. We cannot continue to pretend that our scholarships on competence, skills and fancy concepts make a difference as long as it sees the world as just, balanced and everyone with an equal voice.

57

Underestimating the value of theoretical entanglements and valorizing pedagogical implications instead may divert attention from the very inequalities conditioning how interculturality is unfolding in the real world.

56

There is no grammar of culture. A grammar is for schools and academies. Once we leave these institutions and the cupolas of academies, grammars blow up! Interculturality vomits grammars.

55

I remember my perceptions of western white people as perfectly organized, hardworking and righteous individuals. My explanation of their dominance, as I was a kid, is that god has granted them this status because of their honesty and good deeds. TV, Newspapers and the circulating narratives of Moroccan immigrants showcased Europe as a utopia or 'Jenna' in Moroccan terminology. If one managed to move to Spain or France, for example, then they are saved and living the good life. I gradually started to fathom that their superiority comes at the expense of our conditions, images and self-projection. I started to question this divine privilege that Western societies have had and realized that power inequalities were due to historical political structures and systems. However, my people took that understanding for granted and rarely ever questioned the legitimacy of such a preferential perception of the European other. Interculturality allowed me to see the world for what it is rather than what I have been made to believe it was.

54

Interculturality without race is simplistic, pointless and futile.

53

Interculturality cannot be pinned down, grasped by any one formula.

52

Being 'the underdog' should not be something to take pride in. In certain contexts, being 'the underdog' could be a privilege because it allows one to enunciate some things and be seen as a legitimate spokesperson for others.

51

Asking someone to cite specific authors corresponds to imposing specific ideologies. One should never impose particular authors.

50

Those who preach about interculturality may be the most un-intercultural subjects. [Preaching is dangerous because it sells the illusion that one is among the most intellectually and epistemologically benevolent beings.]

49

Interculturality is interesting as long as you are not at the receiving end of power asymmetries and inequalities.

48

Down with our obsession with seeing students transform into fantasized and solid forms of what we want them to be interculturally! Just let them become and change… *Their change will change.*

47

Asking people to hold off their emotions and feelings in interculturality is a way to 'order' people, to put them back in 'our' place (not theirs), to manipulate them. *Don't have negative thoughts about others; you can't think and/or speak this way.* This makes them feel guilty because what we 'order' them to do is impossible. The guiltier they feel the more controllable they become.

Yet their dark thoughts, their inner *bad*, the backstage of what they do and say remain. These cannot be removed.

All we end up doing is performing ideologies on stage like puppets. The (complex) inner remains.

[Are we training schizophrenics? Are we ourselves schizophrenics?]

46

I am not into drawing this pink imagination of interculturality as well-meaning as a quiet village in Norway; having my laptop and theorizing how people engage with each other and assuming that the world is about identity or essentialism. Everything goes back to coloniality, capitalism, race, discrimination and power asymmetries.

45

Half listened to discussions around a new 'tool' for intercultural dialogue from the 'West' (but pretending to be inclusive of the Global South) yesterday. I heard discourses of 'goodness' and good will, nation-/region-branding, empty discourses, business-like discourses, discourses of social justice... a nice soup of discourses, still dominated however by the overarching 'Western' ideas of democracy and human rights. *Unconvincing.*

44

Western conceptions of art might discredit the originality of non-western creativities since their authenticity may not be commensurated with creative benchmarks in Northern contexts. Such perceptions reproduce the centrality of Northern/Western spaces and the passivity of the colony. The sanctioning of knowledge is still western-based and does not include other perspectives in an equal way. The argument here is that given power imbalances, non-western creativities might be interpreted as derivative or substandard in some cases, if not most of them. That is why communicating creativities should be analysed through the lenses of coloniality of power, knowledge and being (Quijano, 2000; Maldonado-Torres, 2007). Working at the interface of Western and non-Western creativities requires connecting various centres with their peripheries.

43

Stability and a prominent position at a reputable university may sometimes be more important than one's the epistemic rigour of one's scholarships. Academia is not always fair and/or transparent since a lot of decisions are not made on the basis of merit, skills and knowledge.

42

My scholarships are about disrupting linguistic, cultural and epistemic hierarchies which are largely, at least to my understanding, predicated on Western coloniality and cognitive empire. However, I have recently come to realise how much the Global South may be acting within the logics of coloniality. I have noticed how Sub-Saharan individuals are perceived by Moroccans which reflects their re-projection of their own subalternity directed against them by the Global North (e.g., Spain drawing on my own experiences, but I do not generalize since I am referring to some systems and people). It is not an embarrassing situation for me as a scholar who is blaming the Global North for the peripheral contexts' misfortunes, but more of enlightening realization that other dimensions have to be taken within our analyses of power relations. The subaltern may turn into the dominant and the saviour in certain contexts. These south-south power imbalances illuminate how some traditions are not exclusive to some western logics. These are historical dynamics that have existed long ago and will always be there to condition interculturality and human relations.

41

Racialization in creative industries is also persistent and functions precisely in multicultural contexts where ethnic minorities are given little space in the name of social inclusion. For instance, Arab-Australian creative artists were mainly called upon to act as cultural brokers or simply representatives of their communities; Idriss (2016: 406) concluded that "this particular vocational trajectory is indicative of the classed, exclusionary and hierarchical nature of the creative industries". These practices confirm the dynamism and the deployment of long-established power structures across borders through western-centric forms of enunciation and appreciation of the other who is radically different from the Northern contexts. As long as the periphery remains in the shadows, communicating non-western creativities would be a process of re-experiencing the colonial and imperial roots of modernity; this is indicative of how Southern contexts are not central to the production of the modern, only a colonized consumer.

40

It is certainly wrong to invalidate everything that white western scholars have said about interculturality for the sake of visibilizing Southern scholars and theories. This type of colonial praxis would not take interculturality anywhere but only reproduce the same structures and mindsets that we have trying to unsettle and disrupt.

39

Even the topics that should be enunciated through and by the Global South are offered on a silver plate to the Global North. Not only do they own knowledge production infrastructures but also they would take over the Global South's discourses and knowledges.

38

Money is the biggest threat to unthinking interculturality and ridding oneself of our biases and beliefs.

37

Postcoloniality offers the diachronic analysis of sociocultural changes through engagement with constructions of visuality, materiality and conceptions of artistic style and identity (Maihoub, 2015). Postcoloniality makes it possible to examine creativities under the rubrics of how colonial histories have constructed the global taste in arts. Challenging existing Western aesthetic theory is about confronting the centredness of the American-Eurocentric vision. In particular, the monolithic nature of modernity can be challenged by drawing upon hybridity as a postcolonial condition. This necessarily includes examining both the relationality and incommensurabilities among different spaces and how they may come to form equal relationships based on the appreciation of all perspectives regardless of their creative ontology. It is clear that weaving the various contributions of postcoloniality into the discussion on the communication of creativities may grant more visibility to creativity in peripheral places.

36

It remains unclear whether such circumstances may not stymie the development of an artistic vision that is both Southern (local) and modern (Araeen, 2005). Postcolonial nations and states are struggling with legitimacy narratives since knowledge production about art and culture takes place mainly in the West which renders the authenticity of Southern cultural forms to be "legitimized by or in the West (most notably in the art market), these narratives of cultural legitimacy (and the bodies of cultural artefacts on which they are based) carry a lot of weight" (Beurden, 2016: 258–259). For instance, knowledge about Africa and its art continues to be produced in the Global North (Simbao, 2017; Förster et al., 2019).

['Orders' about interculturality]

35

Importantly, Kant's aesthetic theory constructs the idea of the 'subjectively universal' character of aesthetic judgment which largely promotes western-centric perceptions. The modern aesthetic theory in its Kantian forms is not internationally conscious since it contributed to the reproduction of colonialist ideology. It favours Western understandings of universally valid artistic quality and innovation (Danto, 2007). According to Kant, it is only the Germans and the Englishmen who possess "good taste" while those in the Global South lack the good taste as they are impassive, inferior and deficient. To ground any interpretation of artwork on similar notions to Kant's claims of pure aesthetic contemplation, universal validity and good taste is practically the very process of downplaying creativities coming from less global cultures. The premise is, thus, that Southern creativities are aesthetically substandard as they are not able to manifest or demonstrate artistic beauty and ingenuity. Since Kant's singular aesthetic judgment claims self-ascribed universality are inattentive to other views, it is important to consider the glocalism of the contemporary art scene (de Duve, 2007*)* and anchor our analysis of creativities in narratives of globalization and postmodernism by engaging with the particular (singularity, local) and the general (universality, global) (Dimitrakaki, 2012).

34

There are not so many archaeologists of ideas in the broad field of intercul-turality. Our (global) epistemic memory appears to be short-term. We jump at an idea, a concept, a name, an argument and (ab-)use it the same way others do to get into the spotlight (e.g. publish in top journals recycling dominant ideologies). Borders between fields, languages, ideological islands, seem to make us blind in front of the genealogy of ideas, terms and paradigms. What I think is original today might have been obvious, see a cliché, in the past. *Train interculturality archaeologists of the future!*

33

Scholars might draw this abstract idea that classrooms are benevolent and or-ganized spheres with the possibility of applying top-down theories. Moroccan classrooms are different from Finnish classrooms, for example. Teachers' and students' social positionings are quite dissimilar. What is casual and normal for some is a privilege to others. That is why local anchorage should be im-portant in our theorizations as well as explicitly discussing the limitations of our insights because they tend to be "looking from above".

32

Teachers are regarded as patients while scholars are doctors. It would be quite alluring to explore what teachers think of scholars and their theories. Some of the conversations I have had with Moroccan teachers throughout my research have illuminated this aspect. They noted how papers are inac-cessible in terms of language and content. As teachers, they emphasized directness in the sense that they are looking from practicalities and they would appreciate shorter and more straightforward argumentation that ends with a list of possible applications. In particular, intercultural education scholarships are quite complex (recognizing that they are not all complex in the same way) which problematizes teachers' ability to develop practices informed by the relevant literature. One teacher explained how she had no idea what interculturality means in the Moroccan context since literature delivers the perception that cultural diversity functions and manifests in the same way as in Europe and US.

31

The real in-/direct motivation behind any educational approach to intercultur-ality is to make and save money. The fakely humanistic tone one might hear is a decoy. Listen carefully…

30

Interculturality is everything unless it is chopped and dissected to concern only what matters to those in power.

29

Attacking 'commonsense' for saying this or that about interculturality could in fact be disrespectful. Interculturally 'commonsense' has a rich experience. It could be in fact scholars and decision-makers who make us believe in limited understandings of interculturality, in their endeavour to 'grab' it.

28

The unnecessity of moving somewhere else to shine as a scholar is a fact that many Global North academics should certainly be grateful for. It is a massive privilege to stay in one's country around family and friends who are a great part of our lives. They provide help and support which may ultimately be a deciding factor in one's career. Having to apply to other universities for a permanent position, there is always this fear that there may be some complications in terms of visa and taking your spouse with you. The subalternity of the Global South is a real thing; it is not only assumptions and rhetorics.

27

Pushing for non-essentialism is lying to oneself. Closing one's eyes to the inherent contradictions of the human and self. *I say x at moment x and y at moment y.* I adapt to others, contexts, discourses, orders. I disobey. I obey. I lie. I tell the truth.

26

Talking about interculturality is always essentializing it. We make it our own. We try to shape it the way we want it to be. Yet interculturality is not so docile. It escapes us. It tricks us into believing that we trick it.

25

There are different worlds of interculturality. One is in language education which is dominant and the rest are peripheral and limited to certain circles, fields and contexts.

24

Interculturality in language education is often discussed and presented as soft.

23

There are some political tensions between Morocco and Algeria. While they are both at the mercy of European and American forces, they seem to be pushing each other to the edge. Instead of capitalizing on their proximity and earnestly working on consolidating their ties for mutual benefit, they are wasting their resources on conflicts that are unnecessary and unwarranted.

22

Interculturality is also implicated in coloniality. Because it leads apolitical imaginary of human relations, it wrongfully conveys the understanding that people do not systematically subject their fellow humans to grossly unfair treatment and distorted representation. Whenever interculturality is broached, people start devising assumptions about how cultural differences may hamper successful communication. Unfortunately for those seeking to maintain their grip on others' perception of what elements and aspects should be foregrounded, the very attempts to conceal and sugarcoat the world is ardent evidence of how science is an immensely important weapon in perpetuating some people's privilege and others' subordination.

21

It is often essential that we recall the most groundbreaking notions around interculturality such as 'cultural hegemony' which is a concept developed by Italian Marxist Antonio Gramsci. It reminds us how these developed states and ruling capitalist classes make use of cultural institutions (soft power) to consolidate their dominance and control in a world whose dogma is money, status and influence.

20

Emancipation can never undo centuries of intellectual and ontological imprisonment which has made the subaltern imagine an alternative world without the influence and the leadership of those who imprisoned them.

19

The *relativism* argument used to attack those who want to explore other ways of engaging interculturally by admitting that many other ways of considering should stimulate us, appears to be (yet) another way of protecting one's privilege and domination. *It is about the refusal to listen to others.* It is about negating the voice of the other. Relativistic compared to what/ who? Oneself?

18

Interculturality is an illusion to whose charm, beauty and fineness we all contribute.

17

Some of those who passionately and publicly support interculturality may turn out to be the most un-intercultural individuals in their daily lives.

[One of the biggest shocks of my life was traveling with a scholar whom I had admired for a long time – as a reader. During the trips, they kept making racist, stereotypical and 'epistemist' remarks about certain people. Although I was sorely disappointed and upset, I remember thinking that this was a good example of how unpredictable and unstable interculturality could be.]

16

Interculturality exudes a substantial level of patronizing sentiments.

15

It is entertaining to watch politicians *interculturalizing*. Their ways of manoeuvring and dodging are one of the most impressive acts in repudiating our most important taken-for-granted perspectives in interculturality research. Politicians have great 'intercultural competence' because they can certainly make two states whose relations are not characterized by affection look like best friends.

14

Systems of privilege/subordination do not operate in the same ways everywhere. They are neither static nor fixed as they are continuously evolving and taking new shapes and forms. What is subaltern in France could be privilege in Morocco.

13

The one who preaches always thinks that the other is at fault or sinful and therefore responsible for their misfortunes.

12

I strongly support pushing for more equity and justice. However, pushing has to be incremental since pushing too hard will have things to collapse. Allowing the Global South to speak should not be seen as an opportunity to say whatever unless one is naive. Politics are everywhere and pushing has to be wise, systematic, effective and for the long term.

11

We should not ask what works and who (e.g. scholars) are influential; we should ask what works and who (e.g. scholars) gets to be influential – and why.

10

Interculturality could be about everything if the rhetorics are smartly manufactured and manipulated. [Manufacturing here is important: We need to consider whether we are manufacturing complexity and urgency to legitimize our high-brow theories and discourses.]

9

The Global South is colonized to the neck, but our narratives assume the opposite.

8

Current 'orders' about interculturality are either *brief* or *unclear* (and yet rehearsable) so that they can be changed at will. *Just adopt, recycle and recite!*

7

The way we have created stereotypes about interculturality reminds me of our misreading of Chopin's music as 'romantic'. His music is in fact very much about identity struggles rather than romanticism. The key point of interculturality is also the struggles that we experience with ourselves, others, the hyphens between us and this world. Romantic views of togetherness, democracy and tolerance are weak misrepresentations.

6

These dominant discourses around interculturality are painfully adamant. While alternative, complex and political theorizations are produced and shared on regular basis, a lot of people seem to be determined to maintain these easy-to-grasp optimistic representations of interculturality.

5

A Chinese friend shows me email correspondence between himself and a Chinese company organizing English language camps for Chinese children in China. He had messaged them about the fact that they only hired so-called native speakers of English and wanted to find out why. They replied: "when we designed it, it is so". Nothing else. The hierarchy survives. No need for any explanation. Similarly, why is it that 'white' 'Western' scholars like me based at prestigious universities dominate the field of interculturality? "it is (just) so"…

4

African, Asian and Latin American modern and contemporary art has to be included in our understanding of the landscape of global art. To develop a truly global art history, it is necessary to consider the peripheries (Capistrano-Baker, 2015). However, the geographic hub of creativity remains in Europe and North America while imperious historicity continues to limit 'non-Wests' to the 'not yet' (Brown, 2008). That is why including the creativities of regions outside the northern Atlantic spaces remains a sophisticated endeavour. A genuine recognition of non-western artists is an issue even in contexts where multiculturalism, as a framework for managing cultural plurality, is superficially employed to disguise more sophisticated systems of discrimination and disadvantage. Given the absence of any discernible fluctuation of power relations among the Global North and South across spatial spaces, epistemologies or creativities, it might be valid to assume that "cultural, ethnic, and racial differences will be continually commodified and offered up as new dishes to enhance the white palate – that the Other will be eaten, consumed, and forgotten" (hooks, 2006: 380).

3

Gatekeepers in the globalized contemporary art world system "have derived their historical and present power within the globalized art world system from a number of sources that are socio-political, ideological and economic in nature" (Harris, 2013: 536); this is indicative of how the system is a skewed power network controlled by a very limited number of key players.

2

Who am I to tell you that interculturality is this or that when your experience of it might be something completely different [and maybe similar too].

1

Interculturality is definitely not a privilege! *It is everyone's!*

Conclusions

This chapter re-exercises the tradition of critiquing for constructing new vistas and forms of engagements with interculturality. It valorizes the conception of 'mysteries' as normal epistemic dilemmas that attest to the complexities inherited in 'interculturality' as a theory of *everything*. Mysteries are not problems but rather situations where human entanglements are crystallized in the crudest and rawest state of confusion and perplexity. That is, it emphasizes the impossibility of disentangling interculturality from our onto-political positionalities as thinking beings who are constantly producing biased perspectives that simultaneously overfocus and downplay some angles for enunciating. The main takeaway here could be that people are at the nexus of competing interests, complexities and desires that they very endeavour to capture intercultural realities is Sisyphean labour. This chapter supplies a sense of openness towards the unknown as a subject of investigation that is made approachable only when we embrace our lack of sights that is precipitated by our situated narratives and knowledges. These fragments have been imbued with a particular orientation towards exposing our own taken-for-granted perceptions and how we may be re-producing what we critique. We invite the readers to see merit in critique as a fundamental way of knowing as it questions the very tents from which we move forward to think about, understand and interpret interculturality.

[Questions for readers]

- Do you feel that research is a powerful political tool? Isn't the twisting of arguments and rationales a fundamental dimension to all scholarships?
- How do you feel about writers giving you 'orders'? Is it a practice that readers are looking for?
- Are some perspectives inexpressible?
- Is it cumbersome to make substantial efforts to express oneself around interculturality when one could always be misunderstood?
- Assuming that some readers are bilingual and multilingual, is there any language that you feel best conveys your thoughts about interculturality or does language remain deficient and defective?

[Main keywords]

Coloniatellectual: It captures the hegemonic implications in intellectualizing our own power-laden discourses as scholars who are sermonizing and teaching others how to think and act. One may assume that intellectuality is fundamentally innocuous and entirely concerned with knowledge in its most objective form. However, these intellectual discourses may conceal the violence of coloniality through sugar-coated narratives that are presumed to be benevolent and benign. It disrupts the romanticizing of intellectuality and the type of surrealism that often prescribes a good-natured predisposition to our analysis and rhetorics.

Epistemic approval junkies: It argues that scholars may often be inclined to engage in discourses that would ascertain succour by others. Since scholars are bound by certain standards and at the mercy of others (a scholar, official, administrator or politician), they may not be willing to pursue paths that are inherently 'risky' given their political and controversial connotations. While some may be voluntarily an 'epistemic approval junky', there is always a possibility that we subdue our 'true' and 'polemic' opinions in order to survive.

Epistemic positioning: Evaluating knowledges based on the enunciator's stated or inferred geopolitical location and identity. It also speaks of how one may be positioned within a field or sub-field by deriving legitimacy or relevance from their real-life experiences. It is about determining how one's social realities qualify them to enunciate about certain things and ultimately having recourse to these social realities again to assess one's knowledge claims. It may imply that one's spatial, ontological and emotional relationality to knowledge claims is a decisive factor in the appraisal of one's theories, claims and perspectives.

Epistemological risk: Indulging in an unbounded process of knowledge production where one is questioning the very underpinning of 'rationality', 'rigour' and 'robustness'. It is about rejecting to follow the same patterns for navigating and making sense of our social realities taking into account how the 'constructed' discourses would be vehemently critiqued because they are 'unusual' and 'unconventional'.

(The) Fiction of Interculturality: Fiction here denotes that the 'inter' is sometimes imaginary. That is, would interculturality also include the lack thereof? Interculturality may be about negotiating power among us; who is adjusting to the other? who is carrying the burden to please the other? and who decides how that negotiation is taking place?

Looking from above: This is the attitude of making sweeping assumptions about the other's pain, struggles and experiences with a sense of 'teacherhood'. If you were complaining about the train delay while you have your own car, you would probably have to 'presume' and 'imagine' the toll of that on me, but you may again not be interested in understanding it anyway (we used this anecdote because it happened to one of us actually during their studies). There is also "looking from below" where subaltern would cherish and rejoice the very minimum of what others have always taken for granted; for instance, feeling happy about getting a visa confirmed while this is a normal undertaking of the others. If you are looking from below, you would be inclined to aggrandize the other.

Neurosis: It implies the relative loss of touch with reality that accompanies excessive anxiety over some issues. This is a critique of the decolonial that our discourses start to speak us representing our social realities to be entirely driven by our subalternity or usher us to interpret and justify everything based on our geopolitical standing as peripheries. Decoloniality is a narcotic that 'absolves' us and allows us to shirk any responsibility for our conditions.

Opium: This concept was used with regard to 'criticality'. It supplies a false sense of activism that contorts reality and numbs the pain of the less privileged. We may need to identify and unsettle the ways in which criticality limits activism and change to rhetorics promising a fair world that is exclusively lived within the texts. Criticality may have been devised to appease and soothe.

Relationality: It refers to how no person, concept, system or thing exists in isolation since the interactive process with the other is what shapes and defines one's understanding of themselves. Interculturality presents a strong case of relationality in how the 'cultural' self develops in relationship to other 'cultural' selves. However, we are asking here whether relationality might be more accurate than interculturality as an ontological description of these interactive processes. Is interculturality a particular imagination of relationality? Is relationality more inclusive of human communication in that it covers interculturality and moves beyond its epistemological concerns and 'limits'? Are we discussing relationality when we render culture to be 'irrelevant' and 'inconsequential'?

Smokescreen: A cloud of smoke (a ruse) subtly used to conceal other intentions and operations rather than what is visible and announced. It is to deviate, overshadow and distract while maintaining the 'projected' objective to neutrally question, intervene and redress.

Note

1 A note on the inclusion of fragments in the entire book is needed here. In order to make the reading experience even more disruptive and less 'predictable', we have decided to 'number' the fragments in different ways in the chapters: *in reverse order* (Chapter 2), *Roman numerals* (Chapter 3), *Chinese numbers* (Chapter 4).

References

Agamben, G. (2004). *The Open: Man and Animal*. Stanford, CA: Stanford University Press.

Ake, C. (1979). *Social Science as Imperialism: The Theory of Political Development*. Ibadan: Ibadan University Press.

Araeen, R. (2005). Modernity, modernism, and Africa's place in the history of art of our age. *Third Text*, 19(4), 411–417. DOI: 10.1080/09528820500123943.

Atay, A., Eguchi, S., & Nziba Pindi, G. (eds.) (2023). *Translationalizing Critical intercultural Communication: Legacy, Relevance and Future*. Frankfurt: Peter Lang.

Beurden, S. V. (2016). Art, the 'culture complex,' and postcolonial cultural politics in sub-Saharan Africa. *Critical Interventions*, 10(3), 255–260. DOI: 10.1080/19301944.2016.1227216.

Braidotti, R. (1994). *Nomadic Subjects*. New York: Columbia University.

Brown, R. M. (2008). Response: Provincializing modernity: From derivative to foundational. *The Art Bulletin*, 90(4), 555–557. DOI: 10.1080/00043079.2008.10786410

Capistrano-Baker, F. H. (2015). Whither art history in the nonWestern world: Exploring the other('s) art histories. *The Art Bulletin*, 97(3), 246–257. DOI: 10.1080/00043079.2015.1015883.

Crépon, M. (2012). Élections. De la démophobie. Paris: Hermann.

Danto, A. C. (2007). Embodied meanings, isotypes, and aesthetical ideas. *The Journal of Aesthetics and Art Criticism*, 65(1), 121–129.

de Duve, T. (2007). The glocal and the singuniversal. *Third Text*, 21(6), 681–688. DOI: 10.1080/09528820701761095.

de Sousa Santos, B. (2021). *Postcolonialism, Decoloniality, and Epistemologies of the South*. Oxford: Oxford Research Encyclopedia of Literature.

DeMarrais, E., & Robb, J. (2013). Art makes society: An introductory visual essay. *World Art*, 3(1), 3–22. DOI: 10.1080/21500894.2013.782334.

Dervin, F., & Simpson, A. (2021). *Interculturality and the Political within Education* (1st ed.). Oxfordshire: Routledge. https://doi.org/10.4324/9780429471155

Dervin, F. (2022). *Interculturality in fragments: A reflexive approach*. Cham: Springer. https://doi.org/10.1007/978-981-19-5383-5

Dimitrakaki, A. (2012). Art, globalisation and the exhibition form. *Third Text*, 26(3), 305–319. DOI: 10.1080/09528822.2012.679039.

Ennser-Kananen, J. (2019). Are we who we cite? On epistemological injustices, citing practices, and #metoo in academia. *Apples – Journal of Applied Language Studies*, 13(2), 65–69. DOI: 10.17011/apples/urn.201905092524.

Fogarty, T. J. (2009). Show me the money: Academic research as currency. *Accounting Education*, 18(1), 3–6.

Förster, T., Jenni, F., Siegenthaler, F., & Unseld, F. (2019). *Aesthetics of Articulation* (No. 18/19). Institute of Social Anthropology, University of Basel.

Fúnez-Flores, J. I. (2021). Toward a transgressive decolonial hermeneutics in activist education research. In C. E. Matias (Ed.), *The Handbook of Critical Theoretical Research Methods in Education* (pp. 182–198). London: Routledge.

Harris, J. (2013). Gatekeepers, poachers and pests in the globalized contemporary art world system. *Third Text*, 27(4), 536–548. DOI: 10.1080/09528822.2013.810977.

Hart, C. (2011). Legitimizing assertions and the logico-rhetorical module: Evidence and epistemic vigilance in media discourse on immigration. *Discourse Studies*, 13(6), 751–769. DOI: 10.1177/1461445611421360.

Hocking, D. (2018). *Communicating Creativity: The Discursive Facilitation of Creative Activity in Arts*. Basingstoke: Palgrave Macmillan. DOI: 10.1057/978-1-137-55804-6.

hooks, b. (2006). Eating the other: Desire and resistance. In M. G. Durham & D. M. Kellner (Eds.), *Media and Cultural Studies: Keyworks* (pp. 266–280). Revised ed. Oxford: Blackwell Publishing.

Ibelema, M. (2021). *Cultural Chauvinism*. London: Routledge.

Idriss, S. (2016). Racialisation in the creative industries and the Arab-Australian multicultural artist. *Journal of Intercultural Studies*, 37(4), 406–420. DOI: 10.1080/07256868.2016.1190698.

Kristeva, J. (1984). *Powers of Horror. An Essay on Abjection.* New York: Columbia University Press.

Maihoub, A. (2015). Thinking through the sociality of art objects. *Journal of Aesthetics & Culture*, 7(1), 25782. DOI: 10.3402/jac.v7.25782.

Maldonado-Torres, N. (2007). On the coloniality of being. *Cultural Studies*, 21(2–3), 240–270. DOI: 10.1080/09502380601162548.

McCarthy, C., & Dimitriadis, G. (2000). The work of art in the postcolonial imagination. *Discourse: Studies in the Cultural Politics of Education*, 21(1), 59–74. DOI: 10.1080/01596300050005501.

Mignolo, W. D. (2021). *The Politics of Decolonial Investigations.* Durham, NC: Duke University Press.

Quijano, A. (2000). Coloniality of power and eurocentrism in Latin America. *International Sociology*, 15(2), 215–232. DOI: 10.1177/0268580900015002005.

R'boul, H. (2022a). Epistemological plurality in intercultural communication knowledge. *Journal of Multicultural Discourses*, 17(2), 173–188. DOI: 10.1080/17447143.2022.2069784.

R'boul, H. (2022b). Researching the intercultural: solid/liquid interculturality in Moroccan-themed scholarship. *The Journal of North African Studies*, 27(3), 441–462. DOI: 10.1080/13629387.2020.1814750.

R'boul, H. (2023). Intercultivism and alternative knowledges in intercultural education. *Globalisation, Societies and Education*. DOI: 10.1080/14767724.2023.2166018

Samovar, L. A. (1972). *Intercultural Communication: A Reader.* Belmont, CA: Cengage/Wadsworth Publishing.

Simbao, R. (2017). Situating Africa: An alter-geopolitics of knowledge, or Chapungu rises. *African Arts*, 50(2), 1–9. DOI: 10.1162/AFAR_a_00340.

Wittgenstein, L. (2009). *Philosophical Investigations.* London: Wiley-Blackwell.

Yoon, K., Min, W., & Jin, D. Y. (2020). Consuming the contra-flow of K-pop in Spain. *Journal of Intercultural Studies*, 41(2), 132–147. DOI: 10.1080/07256868.2020.1724907.

3   Hesitations and doubts

Introduction

Hesitations and doubts are frequent dilemmas for epistemic subjects in thinking, feeling, sensing and interpreting our experiences. This chapter argues that interculturality is an ontological site where one may be constantly reconsidering their choices, behaviours and stances leading to hesitations and doubts. That is, certainty may allude to epistemic short-sightedness where one is making sweeping claims about how to act interculturally. Why would one be so tempted to think that they have the truth when social realities are immensely complex that even the most renowned scholars in interculturality may struggle to manage a casual intercultural encounter? This chapter presents some profound questioning of our own enunciations as scholars that self-critique is a fundamental exercise for moving forward. Interculturality is uncertainty, hesitations and doubts unless one is eager to subscribe to some comforting perspectives around competence, awareness and training. The fragments exude various senses of describing and engaging with reality that they sketch the different sources of discomfort, exasperation and anger for the authors. The fragments are neither assertive nor oversimplified; the authors may be accused of vacillating attitudes, which could be true, but the premise is speaking oneself is always contingent on our hesitations and doubts. We invite the readers to embrace their confusion and dithering when approaching, navigating and making sense of interculturality.

Five subsections comprise the chapter: [Questioning but no answer], [Sharing doubt and self-critique], [Essai...Erreur... Essai...Erreur], [The inter- can never be equal] and [Why can't cultures just 'die'?]. These subsections engage with multiple topics and issues, but they collectively stress the range of (im-)possibilities in reconciling the complexities inherent in human communication. They also underscore how justice and equity-related discourses are ultimately controversial because they often supply a misleading imagination of how a just world can be truly realized. The fragments also showcase the authors' critique of their scholarships, perceptions and practices in a renewed call for transparency. Some fragments are not only questions

DOI: 10.4324/9781003458050-3

for readers to consider but also (in)direct statements that problematize inter-cultural knowledge and how it is embedded in other topics and fields such as internationalization. This chapter seeks to precipitate further epistemological qualms and demurs.

[Questioning but no answer]

I

If most discussions around interculturality do not centre on culture anymore, then what is the point of 'culturality' in "interculturality" and "intercultural communication"?

[The possibilities to re-brand and de-link from interculturality are limited since they question our 'basic' identities as scholars and educators and could alienate us from potential readers, co-operators and students. If one is not labelled as *intercultural* anymore, one will easily be thrown into another epis-temic and notional silo – while being excluded from the intercultural silo.]

II

Whose interculturality is it in the end? *Mine, yours, ours, theirs...?* When I use the word, can I speak for anyone on the street – a stranger, my baby, an older person in another corner of the world, a wealthy customer at a Chanel store? Most importantly, can I speak for those who meet and experience it? [*A firm no*].

III

How often do we really try to focus on real problems of interculturality in research? Why is it that we seem to look at the notion from a problem-less/fakely problematic perspective? Most of the research that we produce on in-terculturality has nothing to do with real problems but it regurgitates sub-standard and well-rehearsed questions.

IV

Once when I typed in the keywords *colonize + interculturality* in Amazon. com, Byram's (1997) revised book kept coming back as top recommendation.

V

A Chinese student giving a graduation speech at a US university puzzled me. His speech is full of what could be considered as American *ideologemes*. "For when you walk outside that door today, you are already equipped with one of the most critical skills to succeed in the future: the ability to embrace diversity". I wondered how he would phrase this specific ideologeme in Chinese at a graduation ceremony at e.g. Minzu University of China in Beijing. Is regurgitating local ideologemes of interculturality a sign of 'intercultural competence'?

VI

Isn't talking about postcolonial *theory* colonial?

VII

Can interculturality and intersectionality nest? Beyond academic marketing and capitalist ventures, these two are in fact the same…

VIII

How could China ever disengage from the 'West' – unplug – when everything is also very western in the Middle Kingdom?

IX

How I envy people born in China! Their heads seem to be able to navigate between multiple systems:

- Chinese characters-pinyin
- Chinese art/calligraphy/poetry-contemporary art
- Chinese medicine-Western medicine
- The Communist Party-omni-capitalism
- Calls for rationality-omni-superstitions
- Superfluously: chopsticks-forks/knives.

Why isn't my social and intellectual world so liberating?

X

The uncomfortable question: can one seriously engage with interculturality when one speaks one language or a limited range of languages from the same language family and/or ideological contexts? We need to reinvent language.

XI

Can one really decolonize when one only speaks one language? Decolonizing is not just about knowledges but it is also about how we speak within a language and between other languages.

[Interrogate any scholar's engagement with language.]

XII

Are teachers really seen and treated as epistemic subjects and Figures of authority? Scholars tend to position themselves intellectually superior to teachers in the sense they are empty vessels and only workers and implementers of their theories. Teachers need to be perceived through their epistemic capacities. Scholars should aim at designing nuanced frameworks with clear guidelines and allow teachers to make sense of these perspectives and construct their own practices in alignment with their sociocultural spaces and contextual factors. The literature tends to be highly theoretical with little attention to how context is essential in what we say and do.

XIII

I am dreaming of the possibility to view 'bullet chat' (live comments from readers) like on the Chinese Bilibili application on books and articles about interculturality. What do all kinds of others (readers, viewers) think? What critiques do they address to what they read? What contradictions do they face? What is it that they *dis-like*? How could we connect readers and authors in academia in more complex ways?

XIV

Every time I read something about interculturality, how much do I learn about the author rather than *just* interculturality itself?

[Many of us would argue that the author is insignificant and that there is no need to know about them. And yet, knowing about the author is essential in dealing with interculturality and can 'protect' us from their power to speak – often over and for us.]

XV

The idea of community appears to be a substitute for another term at times. Social class, maybe, or even 'race' in some cases?

XVI

What is the real problem of interculturality – if there is one? Have we created illusionary non-problems?

XVII

As a citizen of Morocco, I may have to interculturalize more than others, especially when I am communicating with those who are more privileged. However, the question here is would I have to interculturalize at the same level if I were communicating with someone who is conditioned by more unyielding and overlapping structures of subordination? I may be exercising what I tend to critique against those who are more subaltern than me in a process of redirecting the potential marginalization I feel and/or imagine to the one behind me in the spectrum.

XVIII

(Someone showing off the trips they did abroad during a year on social media) "I can humbly say I am a traveler".

Are you? Is travel as a life-changing, mind-blowing and intellectually challenging process even possible in our capitalistic worlds?

XIX

"Did you find what you were looking for?" What were you looking for? I ask. Were you looking for anything? Maybe there is no need to look for anything *interculturally*?

XX

Would other scholars be ever comfortable making use of knowledges that they regard as untrusted?

XXI

Iris Murdoch (1977: n.p.): "literature mystifies, philosophy clarifies". Interculturality probes?

XXII

I think power is the fundamental priori in social sciences and humanities. All fields would benefit from centring power as a lens for examining, analysing and understanding. Everything going on in the world is because of power; it dictates the winner and loser. It dictates who gets to talk and who is entitled to listen. It dictates who leads and who preys on the illusion of leading but indeed following. Power is what has the world the way it is; moving forward by establishing lacerations within power relations is crucial because differences are limited to the extent where power is a historical fact. It is impossible because then the world would be meaningless. If we both have the same power, then what interculturality are we talking about?

XXIII

Are the differences among people, communities and societies a matter of varying levels of epistemological production or simply contemporary continuations of historical oppressive systems of subordination?

XXIV

I wonder if the Global South was the most advanced now, would they act exactly as the Global North? I am always thinking that Southern countries would commit the same injustices perpetrated by those who are most powerful. Maybe, it is the culture of the dominant, to subalternize, subdue and marginalize. History is actually very telling of how these scenarios have been there through the various eras by different civilizations and empires, especially those who are now in the Global South.

XXV

Use knowledge to question *or* question the use of knowledge?

XXVI

Why is the prefix *trans-* taking over in academic English? Transcultural, translanguaging, transfiction…

XXVII

There is an epistemological dilemma in attending to the decolonization of both the researcher and research (Datta, 2018); is their influence reciprocal? Or is it the researcher who is in charge of decolonizing? I suggest adding the researched as well since these three elements are all impactful creating overlapping systems of privilege/marginalization. I feel that decolonizing is as complex as colonizing is unfolding and continue to shape people's social reality.

XXVIII

For Deleuze and Guattari (2017) there is a difference between a concept and a percept. Percepts have to do with perceptions. They have to do with e.g. how we see and feel things (e.g. in art). Should we talk of the percepts of interculturality rather than its concepts?

XXIX

The majority of exigencies discussed in interculturality are also applicable to all human communication. Then how is interculturality different?

XXX

Which Chinese hotpot are you? Which interculturality are you?

XXXI

Would someone who was born, raised and living in the 'first world' understand interculturality from the perspectives of people from the 'third world' and ultimately engage meaningfully with those perspectives in their scholarships?

XXXII

Asking for someone's origins is also a way of promoting oneself. Who has the power to ask this treacherous question? How much does the question also promote our own (misperceived) 'greatness'? The implicit comparison that the question triggers needs to be revised again and again. Instead of *where are you from?* let's consider the questions *why am I asking this question? Why aren't you initiating this conversation?* But also: *why do I care about this question? Why do I feel I need to ask it?*

XXXIII

Why do I write about interculturality and not other things? Because I feel legitimate to talk about the matters I discuss. Coloniality and decoloniality are all conceptions related directly to my contexts and the experiences that I have had. Interculturality allows me to draw on my geopolitical location to justify what I research and enunciate.

XXXIV

Are all arts intercultural? Are all arts open to intercultural processing? Or are some arts culturally exclusive and they cease to function artistically when they are received outside their situated systems of sense-making, axiologies and ecologies?

XXXV

A job position within intercultural communication based in Europe requires having a 'language profile' involving at least two languages amongst *Dutch, English, French, German, Spanish* and *Italian*. Although most of these languages are used around the world, where are the non-European languages? Does intercultural communication only take place in European languages?

XXXVI

"My name is Zhong Guo but you can call me Eva". *Kindness? Laziness? Coloniality? Reverse power relations? Identity obliteration? Fantasy? Imaginary? Stockholm syndrome? Laxity?...*

XXXVII

Can we really be interested in what is happening *in-between* when we don't have access to this (ungraspable) aspect of interculturality? *Should we stop researching the notion?*

XXXVIII

Does interculturality make sense to those who are on the lower spectrum of being? Those who only listen but do not talk? Those who only read but do not write? Those who are taught but do not preach? Those who are commanded but do not order? Those who follow but do not lead?

XXXIX

An interesting question that captures the amalgamation of skewed geopolitics of knowledge and language is: Would the prominent theories and scholars in interculturality have the same acclaim and impact if they wrote their works in languages other than English? Any imagination of knowledge production and consumption that turns the back to the seriousness of their response to this particular question is denying the very premise of what modern science looks like. This question needs to be taken as the essential principle in any perspective/research on epistemology and knowledge production. It is a question but we all know the dreadfulness of the response because it might entail the destruction of our very romanticizing perception of epistemology, knowledge and voice.

XL

Is the very fact that some intercultural scholars may not have substantial intercultural experiences in the sense that they have engaged with perspectives, knowledges and ontologies that do not bear much resemblance to their own situated understandings either through travel, work or research, epistemologically correct and veracious? Isn't it problematic that we may be running the risk of theorizing what we have not experienced? To what extent do our narratives derive their legitimacy from our own lived experiences? Can the narratives that are not grounded in real-life experience be also perceived as real, original and innovative or they are mere productions of logical and imaginative extensions?

XLI

Could culture be designated as a civilization? Was culture the first true instance of civilization? if so, then it opens up the opportunity to make a case for how some cultures are more civilized than others although again civilization can be relative. We may be both civilized but in different forms.

XLII

Working on interculturality in education and research must always serve to redefine us. How is my research also changing and interculturalizing me?

XLIII

Maybe scholars are concerned that once decolonial, critical and political social justice-oriented discourses have obtained an essential role in intercultural communication education and research, the dominant narratives and knowledges would be sidelined. The concerns to keep some discourses alive and mainstream may be at the expense of the field moving forward. However, it is expected that the truly critical turn that derives its legitimacy from unravelling power relations would pervade at a certain time. Certain populations may not find answers to their questions and ultimately start opening up new channels of thought that centre their issues. What value can be found in continuing to vouch for what does not involve me and delivers the impression that I am responsible for my own subalternity and I should make the required efforts to change that because that is not their business?

XLIV

Writing from my small room in a small city somewhere in the Global South and preaching about power hierarchies like a little boy whose candy was taken by his schoolboys and calling for some turns in interculturality research and education is a great exemplification of not only epistemic dissonance but also how powerful words may be (I assume my words may have some power, but again this may be due to some exaggerated self-confidence). Yet, I always ask myself: who am I to be suggesting what to be done? I may sound like a little bird tweeting and singling in the early morning and only two or three people listening carefully and enjoying the rhythm. That bird needs a bigger stage and audience otherwise it sounds like it is singing for itself. Most of the time it is not entirely about what is being sung but who sings what. [While my tweeting may not appeal to certain ears, I refuse to be signing the whims of others whose rhythms and lyrics feel incommensurate with my experiences; would someone living in the countryside in Morocco be listening to opera? I do not think so.]

XLV

Why do we give intercultural lessons to others? Can we be so good at it ourselves that we can lecture them? Anyone can 'do' interculturality, and, often, much better than 'us'!

[Sharing doubt and self-critique]

XLVI

Chinese 'religions' have to do with the philosophico-religious and the ethico-religious. Seeing someone put their hands together at a Buddhist temple in China does not mean that they are 'praying' or engaging in any 'religious' activity. Maybe like the Proto-Indo European root of *pray*, *prek- indicates, they might just be *asking, requesting, pleading*.

XLVII

"Invest in yourself. Invest in interculturality". The more they teach it to you, the less ready you will be! Interculturality is nothing to be ready for. It is ready before us.

XLVIII

Interesting to note that many Chinese people mis-use the word *community* for *communist* in English. Similarly, I have seen words like *intertextuality* and *intersectionality* being used instead of *interculturality* in English. Although these were most probably slips, one cannot but think of the thin line between these different notions.

XLIX

There should be a constant voice whispering to us that we are not doing and cannot do it right in intercultural research and education.

L

My mind must be available. Leave space for other ways of thinking, mixing with what's already there. I cannot continue to bury myself in my own mud.

LI

Encounters with selves by way of alterity is my (temporary) definition of interculturality today. 20.8.2022. (FD).

LII

In January 2022, someone tells me: "I hope that after these past three years, we can all go back to normal". But aren't power relations, selfishness, conflicts and lies, as witnessed during the pandemic, part of the *normal*?

LIII

I feel frustrated and yet relieved at the fact that language cannot allow me to speak about interculturality.

LIV

We need to feel strange and astonished in front of research on interculturality.

LV

Democratic culture and Intercultural Competence.
   Ideological intimidation?

LVI

I am an academic because I am an artist (and vice versa). The frustration of not being able to create satisfactorily on canvass, I am delighted to put on paper as a writer. The joy of seeing art replacing words from time to time. Art and research could offer a balance for each other.

LVII

A Chinese artist friend shows me a painting of a person whom I imagine to be an old female farmer in a field. She reminds me of a friend's mother whom I had met years ago. She had this kind of 'frozen' smile that seemed to reveal hidden pain to my eyes. "This is a madman", my artist friend says. We then spend an hour discussing different elements from the painting, trying indirectly to convince each other of what we see. But only him knows what the painting is about. As a viewer, I am allowed to see who I want to see, to link them up to my own life visions, experiences, to that complex invisible intertextuality that composes our lives. Interculturality is the same. We push and pull. But there is no winner. There should not be. This hesitation could be at the core of interculturality.

LVIII

Oppose and compare fantasy (personal perspectives) and imagination (imposed by others) in intercultural work.

LIX

Interculturality as a subaltern is totally different from interculturality as a privilege. I am a subaltern, I always feel the need to discuss power, not intersubjectivity because it explains but does not amend my position within the lower spectrum of intercultural encounters.

LX

Power is what pressures me to recognize your existence on one hand. But, on the other hand, it allows you to live stress-free even when you do not recognize my existence.

LXI

Hong Kong caused me to doubt what I have known and learned. The fast pace of life is not something I am used to but that is part of interculturality; moving beyond what we know and being willing to listen and learn without judging.

What works for me may not work for others but this is not a standard for what is better or worse.

LXII

I, myself, do not feel always capable of successfully navigating intercultural encounters despite my scholarships. Sometimes, that success is contingent on my willingness to compromise myself and appeal to other's logics and ways of handling things (R'boul, 2022). I often have to explain how I am from Morocco, and how I do not know some things and/or how they could be done. The very fact that I mention Morocco is very reflective of how I blame my home country for my shortcomings. Maybe, this could be real but the very fact that I have to mention it to explain is very telling of power dynamics.

LXIII

I have heard once that the west has reached its fullest potential while there is a lot of improvement for the Global South. I am not sure of the accuracy of this claim since the west could always appropriate the 'advance' taking place in the periphery.

[China seems to be running after 'development' and 'enrichment' and I have felt that these ideologemes are often embedded in discussions of interculturality in the Middle kingdom too. When I once asked a friend what 'civilized' or 'developed' meant to them, they referred to how the 'West' was a model for development: good education, welfare, happiness, politeness... I was quick to respond that I was not sure that 'we' had any of these and that the 'West' is such a diverse (imaginary) place (compare e.g., Finland and the UK)... It is hard for me to imagine how and why someone would look up to the 'West'. Trying to place myself in their shoes remains impossible. I am including Figure 3.1 here to showcase a form of contradiction that I have often witnessed in the Chinese context. The picture shows a poster promoting 'Chinese campus culture of the dining room' (as put in English on the poster) at a university canteen in Beijing. However, as the reader will notice, the illustrating picture on the poster contains mostly 'Western' cheeses, somehow contradicting the 'Chineseness' of the advertised food.]

LXIV

I have always been hesitant to affirm the epistemological legitimacy of arts of extending our understandings of interculturality under the premises that rationality and logic are the way forward. However, as Fred shared some snapshots from his forthcoming book about art and interculturality; he managed to brilliantly convince me of the relevance of arts in interculturality as the

校园食堂文明

放心健康

新 鲜　营 养　分 享

CHINESE CAMPUS CULTURE OF THE DINING ROOM

校园文化 食堂文明

谈到中国饮食文化，许多人会对中国食谱以及中国菜的色、香、味、形赞不绝口。但是
如果要从比较的角度来探讨饮食文化，可以操作的办法是把握住中国饮食文化的精髓。
没有比较就没有鉴别。笔者在这里认为，比较可行的办法是在讨论中国饮食文化时，
从饮食生活方式的角度来着手。

Figure 3.1 Poster promoting 'Chinese food' at a university canteen in Beijing

paintings used could be visibly linked to the ideas discussed. Arts are alternative modes of knowledge production and I am in support of this attitude of renovation and seeking other profound modalities of engagement to move forward. What I have learned the most from Fred is to dare to challenge, question and offer new ways of thinking.

[The same obviously applies to Hamza's mind-blowing contributions.]

LXV

I am not sure whether the objective of interculturality is to explain or change. Maybe, it could do them both or neither of them. It all depends on what is being said, but it depends more on who said it. The very politics of enunciation does not promise change unless the ones who got to enunciate refrain from preaching.

LXVI

"The more you analyse music, the more mysterious it becomes" (French composer and teacher Nadia Boulanger, 1887–1979). Pastiche: *the more you analyse interculturality, the more mysterious it becomes.*

LXVII

It is virtually impossible to imagine a world where systems of privilege/subordination are annulled. Within the logics of the world, these systems might be necessary for our race's development since they create dynamics by which certain people get to evolve and ones are forced to follow.

LXVIII

Place a distance between what you see and your potential experience of it!

LXIX

During my doctoral studies, I was not allowed to access universities and high schools unless I went to the ministry of education and asked for permission. I did so only to be told by the ministry that the local directorates are responsible for this. As I went back again, there were multiple hurdles simply because I was a PhD student at a foreign university. I was asking myself whether I look like a spy or appropriating data that I was not entitled to. I am sharing this incident just to point out how we need to look at ourselves before others. Decoloniality might be misleading in the sense that it deflects our attention to blame others instead of looking at our own philosophies, thinkings and practices. [It is important that this is not construed as blaming the subaltern for their subalternity; there is a fine line between being honest (peeling oneself) and seeking to critique for the sake of critique. Our critiques cannot simply fill books on duty shelves because they have to name; they have to allow us to have our fingers on the wounds.]

LXX

What you say is not always *you who said it* but probably what others said through you in ways that fool you to believe that it is you who are saying it.

LXXI

Someone asks me about something I have said in an interview in 2017: "what do you think about that?". I reply that I don't remember saying that and that I was probably filling up time orally. I don't agree at all with what I was reported to have said.

[Disagree with yourself.]

LXXII

Some notions in interculturality such as *tolerance, equality* and *diversity* are great examples of politics of distraction. These notions are convenient and bear little relevance to power asymmetries, yet they are widely endorsed and celebrated. We need to ask whether these politics of distraction are intentional or simply effects of some people's self-ascribed universality of knowledge and their imaginative extensions of their logics as they were to apply in other contexts.

LXXIII

Epistemic dissonance is an interesting conception that captures the (im)possibilities of decentring interventions into global knowledge production. It refers to "cognitive and behavioural inconveniences resulting from situations in which scientists and practitioners are expected to accept and act upon information obtained by untrusted epistemologies" (Raška, 2022: 2). In interculturality, which is supposedly expected to manifest a genuine intercultural exchange of knowledges, epistemic dissonance can be used to understand how the experiences of others could be appropriated under the implicit assumption that knowledges of others about themselves may not accurate and/or legitimate since they are untrusted epistemologies. Also, it could also imply how the under-representation and invisibility of Southern epistemologies may not be due to the deliberate process of overshadowing alternative knowledges but it is simply due to the fact that the Global North does not believe in the epistemic capacity of those ways of knowing. I think the dominant discourses in decoloniality have already made the presupposition that the Global South believes that epistemologies of the South are trusted epistemologies and, therefore, the next step is to foreground them, but the case might be that the western cognitive empire does not even agree that Southern perspectives have anything to offer. The sympathy of some northern parties to allow the subaltern to speak may be out of their political campaigns and rationales rather than actual belief in the epistemic originality and significance of Southern epistemologies.

LXXIV

When we write about interculturality, we should not pretend to give away everything, 'solutions' to problems but entice our readers to dig into these issues for themselves. For them to find problems concerning interculturality is already a victory for the writer.

[A book should never be self-sufficient.]

LXXV

I usually ask my students and friends if they think that Moroccans are racist. They often answer that we are not because their understanding of racism is based on the mainstream imagination of the discrimination inflicted upon some black people by some whites. Then, I steer the discussion to examine further how we are self-racializing by using certain notions and words to describe others and ourselves.

LXXVI

Reading on a bench in a park in China:

"Excuse me!"
I hear but I don't look.
"Excuse me!"
I raise my head and reply: "yes, hi, do I know you?"
"No"
"Sorry, I must focus on my reading now. Bye."

I feel guilty again for doing this. Should I address a mere stranger who approaches me? Am I a bad person? Should I accept to play the game of what I always imagine will be a meaningless interaction? Exchange a few words: *where are you from? How do you like China? Bye*. Why not give it a try? Let things happen?

[Essai...Erreur... Essai...Erreur]

LXXVII

Sleepwalking as a double-sword word for interculturality as an object of research and education. I sleepwalk through interculturality to open my eyes. I let my mind roam and like a bee 'gather nectar' *here and there*, ideas, knowledges, discourses, words, ideologies... Like in a dream, I let myself dare to try anything. I can also sleepwalk through interculturality when I close my eyes to other ways of perceiving, 'tasting' and seeing the notion – without being interested in other ways of thinking about it, closing my eyes to the problems of inequality, racism, the Global South, etc.

LXXVIII

Interculturality must be an apple of discord.

LXXIX

Someone told me that my art 'smells of music!'. *Disrupt senses!*

LXXX

Interculturality would benefit from a novel philosophical identity that valorizes constant critique and questioning in a world where realities are plural and continue to pluralize.

LXXXI

Maybe if the world was equal, we would have totally different ontologies, ecologies and epistemologies. We would have a completely different unfolding of daily life. Maybe inequalities are what push us forward to think, reflect and question.

LXXXII

It would be interesting to examine the syllabus used to teach intercultural communication/education or those courses that claim to embrace the premises and objectives of intercultural education. The mesmerizing regularity through which our discourses are imbued with this sense that we actually implement what we preach.

LXXXIII

Our ideas may be often strategic more than the outcomes of our true intellectual labour. That is, we may say something because it gets us somewhere and we may not say something because it may get us somewhere, we do not desire. [This is more dangerous that being sidelined and silenced: the very act of enunciating to please and conform.]

LXXXIV

What does intercultural education mean in a peripheral context such as Morocco? Interculturality research and intercultural education have not said much about these spheres since little has been theorized and examined about what interculturality is unfolding in these spaces. Identity, self and other would certainly be exciting topics to unravel but these countries are at the exteriority of modernity that they are looking from a small window into the world. They are still struggling to catch up and assert the legitimacy of their voices, ontologies and knowledges. They are never in a position of power unless they are dealing with other peripheral contexts in Africa, for example. We, scholars, concentrate on what comes as handy and apolitical; we like to see the world through overly positive lenses. We assume things and we jump to conclusions that sometimes make no sense to some people. Theories remain theories unless they materialize some activism, honesty and directness, and most importantly reflect vehement support for justice.

LXXXV

I wonder if I were 'British' or 'American', would I be speaking and writing about the same things?

LXXXVI

We could also be wondering if eminent intercultural scholars were Moroccans, would they be speaking and writing about the same things?

LXXXVII

It would be interesting to explore how both scholars and teachers perceive these conceptual pluralities in interculturality. Do we really need 'intercultural', 'transcultural', 'multicultural' and 'cross-cultural' to speak of intercultural relations, or are they endeavours to fake genuine contributions to the field? It may feel that scholars are writing and feeding themselves if not other scholars who completely subscribe and blindly endorse their ideas. It may be safe to predict that teachers would face some difficulties to make sense of all these notions since they all sound the same unless there are some nuances that only those who use them are aware of. They also create a condition in which we are immensely preoccupied with the concepts and words we are using that we ignore how we are using these notions to construct our knowledge and meaning. Scholars need to make use of these notions not being used and consumed by them. Notions are not temples, holy revelations or prophetical enunciations.

LXXXVIII

Essai... Erreur... Essai... Erreur... Essai... Erreur... Essai... Erreur...
Essai... Erreur... Essai... Erreur...
Essai... Erreur... Essai... Erreur...
Essai... Erreur... Essai... Erreur...
Essai... Erreur... Essai... Erreur...

LXXXIX

It is important to ask questions to which we do not yet know the answers. [It is also important not to presume having answers to all questions: the value of some questions resides in their un-answerability. Those unanswerable questions are fundamental to keep thinking.]

XC

Academia can be a tricky and appalling experience if one is not drawing on the tools of the dominant. There are some unwritten rules that everybody is expected to abide by. Is it really only about one's epistemic and scientific rigour or also about one's race, colour and nationality? Even those who manifest vehement critiques of nepotism and whiteness in academia may be complicit in the system of white supremacy.

XCI

I wonder how interculturality would be if there were no power asymmetries and inequalities. Would interculturality be meaningful? Would interculturality even matter? Would it be still called interculturality? Would interculturality be dominated by the same perspectives we have had before and now?

[Would it even be an impossible possibility?]

XCII

A colleague asked me whether I genuinely believe that my scholarships of decolonization and inequalities within knowledge production are making any difference. It was a disturbingly poignant question that would easily lead to an existential crisis. My reply was that "I am not that naïve to think that, but I am confident that my papers are drawing some people's attention to these issues which can then induce a larger impact. Shedding the lights on these injustices is possible, but decolonization is far-fetched".

XCIII

Reading most research on interculturality, I feel alienated. *This is not what I feel I experience; this does not sound like interculturality to me.* Am I experiencing an impostor syndrome? Am I an impostor?

XCIV

What academia would look like if the major publishers and prestigious journals were based in Africa and run by African editors? Postcolonial and decolonial scholarships would finally be legitimately led by the Global North. [We may have cases of black scholars as experts in white studies; privileged Africans living in high-rise flats in Tunis as experts in subaltern studies that centre the hardships of people in the Anglo-sphere.]

XCV

The global movement has become a must and taken-for-granted condition in academia. We never ask questions about how these movements are influencing scholars' voices and scholarships. What makes some scholars be welcomed in the Global North and not others? What parameters qualify a scholar to be employable by the Global North?

XCVI

How many people experiencing interculturality are not allowed to speak about it the way it speaks to them? How many are silenced in research and education?

XCVII

Writing about and researching interculturality is like fighting against a ghost, a non-being at times. Who/what is it that we are talking about? I see the word everywhere but I don't feel its presence.

XCVIII

Am I allowed to judge people in other contexts who only befriend those who can benefit them and ignore/avoid others? Am I allowed to judge people in other contexts who cheat their ways through the system by abusing others? 'Their' system, which requires unrealistic outcomes, seems to push them to do so – and many are successful at it! *Save your skin, protect your own people, get benefits, survive.* As someone who does not have the same pressure in his life and relations, it is hard to accept. However, I am very much aware that I would probably act the same way if I had been *un-privileged* to be part of that system.

XCIX

One can always decide not to play the game. One can always decide to lose. One can always accept to be a nobody.

C

Misleading identity-making from a scholar? "I don't work on language, I work on communication". What's the difference? Is communication without any form of language possible?

CI

It is amazing how our perspectives can shift when we are critiqued. We are suddenly oppressed, overshadowed and invisibilized. [This is very tricky: I am bit surprised that I wrote this because I am offering ready-made critique against my own scholarships; critiquing oneself is bittersweet because I am not sure whether I am slapping and kissing at the same time to tickle others to appreciate what I say.]

CII

Pianist Anne Queffelec (2016: n.p.) refuses to describe a piece by Handel, arguing that music talks to us 'beyond words'. Music gives us 'electric shocks', which words cannot express. One could say that interculturality does the same to us. So why try to describe it *in words*?

[The paradox of writing so many books and articles. This very question questions any question.]

CIII

We don't have to help others understand or 'do' interculturality. Do we ourselves understand or know how to do it? What we can do is support others in realizing and accepting that interculturality is not a 'thing' out there to be grabbed! But they already probably know about this...

CIV

I see someone pray in front of a Chinese character that refers to some Buddhist Figure. There is no physical representation of that Figure. I wonder what it would feel like to see someone pray in front of the word GOD instead of a statue of Jesus.

CV

Heard: "The more I communicate with foreigners, the more I learn about interculturality". Do I *really*?

CVI

With all these portfolios and logbooks of interculturality being produced in education, we could wallpaper the whole world. The thing is who would read them? What do teachers and students do with them? What is the real goal of all this writing?

CVII

Can we think un-westercentrically while everything we have, watch, listen, read and write is anchored in western logics of creativity, logic and rationality? It may be virtually impossible to distance oneself from what has been the encompassing ontology and epistemology. I am not optimistic that non-western epistemologies would materialize one day as a pure, fine and unadulterated form of knowledge production. We defend and support epistemologies of the South in ways that make sense for the Global North. I discuss decoloniality within interculturality in ways that appeal to western institutions, outlets and scholars' reasonings. It is not heroic to lead a false conviction that one can confidently and systematically abstract away from western knowledges.

CVIII

Repeating oneself is healthy; why should I say what I do not believe in? Why should not I repeat what hasn't been heard? I will stop repeating myself when what I have said has been heard and taken into account. Shouldn't we all shout *again* when the other person cannot hear us and look our way? [Having to repeat oneself is probably because one has not been heard yet; or, they are probably repeating the only thing that has been ever heard.]

CIX

This tendency to try to make 'things' look scientific in intercultural research is exhausting. I see e.g. the abbreviation IaH being used for the 'concept' of Internationalization at Home – trying to make it look like a concept from physics or biology. But is it a concept at all? Does it ask any question? Does it make us think?

CX

This sloganesque 'order' seen on WeChat and heard in different academic situations: "It's important to embrace diversity". *Naivety and emptiness*. What diversity are we talking about? Is the idea of embracing (from Greek *brakhion* for *an arm*) inclusive and reciprocal enough? Isn't there a risk that the suggested embrace lead to one-way decisions and thus to increasing inequality? I decide to embrace you, to move my arm forward to you, as someone I consider 'diverse' but what about you? What if you reject my embrace? What if you feel looked down upon by my embrace? Can you also make the decision to embrace me if I am in a superior position?

CXI

Isn't a non-normative model of interculturality the worst oxymoron and white lie? I would not be surprised if ethics was also mentioned as having guided the 'creation' of such a 'model'…

[The inter- can never be equal]

CXII

The idea of competence is particularly irrational to me. Competence is certainly an outstanding case of epistemic stretch. Instead of opening up our discourses to more complexity that is reflective of reality, they simply choose to debate the same normative notions and perspectives. How competence would be relevant to an African immigrant who is living undocumented in Europe? Does competence even have anything to say about this type of interculturality? Interculturality is not a hard science and would never be. We either realistically examine its manifestations without these hegemonic knowledges that present self-ascribed internationality of certain types of interculturality in certain contexts as global facts all over the world. Everybody should be allowed to theorize interculturality in ways that make sense to them, but it should be noted that these ideas are contextual and limited to certain situations and spaces.

CXIII

When power asymmetries are adamant, the only possibility left for interculturality is to be examined by means of the unfolding dynamics through which negotiation and co-construction of meaning do not necessarily mean reciprocity.

CXIV

Interculturality can never and never will be about equality. The *inter-* can never be equal, even in the utopias that we have constructed in our tired worlds.

[When a word becomes a slogan, we lose hope.]

CXV

Today someone claimed (again) that my work could lead to *relativism*. But relativism for whom and from what perspective? To relativize you need a gauge... who is that gauge for the 'Western' scholar who warns me against relativism? Do we know enough about other ways of doing interculturality to close the door to other 'options'? To relativize shares the same root as to *relate, relation*. Before deciding if we are relativizing wrongly, let's listen to others, question ourselves, be(come) with others. To accuse someone of relativizing without these is to reveal too much about one's own ideological indoctrination... *Relativism as an alibi?*

CXVI

Would we ask a teacher or a scholar directly to provide advice about how to be a (good, real) human being? *So why do we ask them for advice about being intercultural?*

CXVII

A reviewer of one of my papers on Chinese Minzu education criticizes the fact that references to American multiculturalist scholar James Banks and British multiculturalist Modood are not to be found in the paper. Why would we need these voices to talk about Chinese education? Would the same reviewer be critical of a paper on American education that fails to refer to Sude or Teng (two specialists of Chinese Minzu education)?

CXVIII

What does intercultural education, which is a Euro-Americano construct, mean for African peripheries? What epistemological unlearning and deconstruction can be applied to reimagine intercultural education in ways that account for Africa's intimacies, needs and objectives? By unsettling the political structuring of educational theories, we can build on the linguistic, cultural and epistemic relationalities among African spaces' postcolonial positionings and their collective aspirations for decolonial praxis and epistemic emancipation.

CXIX

Interculturality is a philosophical abyss: Fragmented, ambivalent and subjective.

CXX

Someone once told me that "you are always going to be 'something' in the eyes" meaning that you are always going to be framed either by your gender, nationality, race or culture.

CXXI

No one can specialize in interculturality but everybody is a specialist of it.

CXXII

Interculturality must belong to common people rather than to researchers exclusively. [This makes no sense. It cannot but belong to common people.]

CXXIII

Can one be an interculturalist without being a *flaneur* strolling through books, music, art, ideas, debates, images, etc.?

[After reading a research paper or a book, go to an art museum, sit on a bench in a park and open your eyes, ears and breathe in.]

CXXIV

"To be honest…". *How could you?* You are a scholar and/or an educator embedded in a hyper-capitalistic system.

CXXV

I hope I am not perceived by others that I am preaching and only complaining. My hope does not stem from my concern about seeking others' approval but from my concern that their perception may thwart the understanding of my texts and arguments as I imagine them.

CXXVI

It is not possible to construct alternative worlds, only alternative understandings of the world.

CXXVII

Researching and educating for interculturality should be done beyond culpabilization. Making others feel guilty about what they do, think, produce, disseminate, experience, argue goes against interculturality.

[But isn't it what I have done myself in my own writings?]

[Can one engage in scholarship and education about interculturality beyond guilt?]

CXXVIII

Researching interculturality should be both a destructive and [partially] creative act.

CXXIX

Online interactions between a group of students based in China and a group of international students in Finland. One of the students in Finland places the words 'Leave Taiwan alone' on his ID bubble instead of a picture. The Chinese are shocked and somewhat angered. During the meeting, the students were planning to discuss future online encounters around education for emergencies.

Intercultural sabotage in a space that was meant to be 'safe'.

What to do?

This is real interculturality beyond the happy and shiny. This is interculturality as politics.

Speak.

CXXX

If interculturality is a bridge, we do not cross to any of the sides but stay together, balancing in the centre of the pathway of the structure. We are fated to stay there together.

CXXXI

Wearing financial glasses when working on interculturality should be compulsory! How much are we worth alone and together? What benefits do we get from others, and each other? (The unspoken).

CXXXII

Maybe there is physically one world, but certainly countless versions of that world in our minds and psyches. [This could be patronizing that one is stuck in a cage that they decide to paint it; those who have been in a cage for a while, they ended up thinking flying is forbidden. I may have said this somewhere else, but it is always worth re-mentioning.]

CXXXIII

Walking at my favourite park in China in freezing temperatures, I suddenly hear a piece of music called *Cantus Arcticus* by Finnish composer Eino-Juhani Rautavaara (1928–2016) on my phone. The piece describes the arctic and includes recording of birds from a specific region of Finland. What a strange coincidence leading to two different locations being suddenly merged into one: the view of a frozen lake, a chilling sensation on my skin because of the freezing wind and a sensory experience that brings me back to Finland. Interculturality and the more than human in supersensory ways!

CXXXIV

Explore the idea of *capitalist militarism* (Mann, 1984) for intercultural research and education. We are placed in a constant state of 'exceptionalism': But who decides? For what reasons? What does it do to the underprivileged? And what does this state allow the powerful to do to themselves?

CXXXV

Why is it that we seem to be fascinated by the power and strength of crowds? This uncontrollable 'animal'? The crowd is always there, it is part of us, inside of us. It controls us. It forces us to think and speak. The gregarious, the anonymous and yet doxic in all of us! Moussaid (2021) talks of *crowdoscopy* (the study of crowds). Intercultural research and education should introduce us to this field! So much of what we say and think about the notion is gregarious.

CXXXVI

Working on basic concepts for interculturality I wonder: what is it that we are talking about? What is *that* interculturality? Is it a ghost?

CXXXVII

If I don't like an English first name that a Chinese person has chosen to use [a sign of 'neo-colonialism' to me; a sign of kindness and generosity towards non-Chinese, many Chinese say], do I have to use it? Shouldn't I make an effort in any case to learn all names – Chinese ones included?

[Why can't cultures just 'die'?]

CXXXVIII

Does interculturality research do enough for the subaltern? Does interculturality centre what is not communicative but rather ontological? These questions present epistemological dilemmas for the fields. [Maybe people do not want to see these inequalities because it reminds them of how privilege they are; they downplay their complaints.]

CXXXIX

I have grown up in a way that as much as I laughed, I expected to feel the opposite the next day. A feeling of guilt starts to seep into me whenever I am happy because I may have learned that that's not the normal situation. The normal is to feel nothing or simply cannot situate oneself in a feeling that could be described to others.

CXL

I have been writing about interculturality, but I am always stressed whenever I am engaging in intercultural encounters. No matter what I know about interculturality, I realize that I do not know enough to actually navigate intercultural relations without an inherent sense of doubt and uncertainty. Maybe, I would never know enough to do that, or maybe it is not about knowledge but lack of knowledge to simply not care and proceed in whatever ways one's positionality allows them to. This gap between knowledge and reality is a reminder of the complexity of interculturality and intercultural encounters.

CXLI

Writing fragments does not mean I am of the same calibre as Cioran. Maybe better, maybe not!

CXLII

How relevant is interculturality for arts? Could we exercise interculturality through arts or arts through interculturality, or are they in interplay to make sense of navigating each other?

CXLIII

The theory of cognitive dissonance refers to "inconsistency between beliefs or behaviours creates an aversive motivational state akin to hunger or thirst. This tension is typically reduced by changing one of the dissonant elements, or adding new ones, until mental consonance is achieved" (Cooper & Carlsmith, 2015: 76). It describes "a motivational state that impels the individual to attempt to reduce and eliminate it. Because dissonance arises from inconsistent knowledge, it can be reduced by decreasing or eliminating the inconsistency" (Wicklund & Brehm, 1976:1); I have felt this dissonance multiple times whenever I am drawing comparisons between what I believe, what I say and what I do. It is not an acknowledgement of being fake or a hypocrite, but more of a realization of how reality is complex and how our scholarships tend to assume that these complexities are well-captured.

[Scholars and educators are liars, performers and manipulators too.]

CXLIV

Would cultures die one day? Would all of us have one set of knowledges, ontologies and ecologies? I do think so. If western dominance continues for thousands of years, the other nations would be gradually moving towards the norms and understandings dominant in these places. I see that genuine transformation in Morocco and how people are becoming and consciously endeavouring to sound and look like idealized others.

CXLV

He is not really a sociologist or an educationalist either. He is a linguist – thrown in like an insult! *He is not really Finnish. His family is from western Europe. Dervin is a particular name for a Finn.* Trying to deauthorize authority, attempting to put down my ideas. *As if saying: he does not know what he is talking about interculturally. He is a fraud.*

[And still this unfortunate incident in Italy.]

CXLVI

I feel frustrated and yet relieved at the fact that language cannot allow me to speak about interculturality.

CXLVII

Listening to a Finnish colleague talking about diversity, I wonder: If we speak about interculturality in ways that others do not understand – using specific glocal and polysemic ideologemes – how could we do interculturality among scholars too? How to balance 'global' (i.e. Western dominated) and local *interculturemes*?

[We apologize to the reader for using many such elements in this book. We hope that the fragmentary nature of our writing can serve as an excuse while urging you to 'dig' deeper into our interculturemes for yourself.]

CXLVIII

The joy when I realize that I do not understand and cannot translate a word! Like a jigsaw puzzle, I look at the piece, turn it around several times. Often, it does not belong to the puzzle. I ask the others' eyes, ears and mouths to flip it around too, to whisper its flavours, to add spices and sweets. When I think I understand the word – or, rather, that I can taste it – it escapes from me again.

CXLIX

Why do I feel so uncomfortable seeing my art at a gallery? [I don't feel the same about my writing.] I tell a friend that art is too personal. It reveals too much. My friend replies: "but everything is personal… your writing included".

CL

Interculturality must forget itself while remembering its simplexity.

CLI

Hell is the other people, but the same argument could be made for heaven. People oscillate between these two places in inexplicable ways. [What about feeling heaven as a hell and feeling hell as heaven?]

CLII

We often write when we are not in the mood for it. We often write what we do not believe in for the sake of political correctness.

CLIII

As much as hell is the other people, we are hell to them as well.

CLIV

Wittgenstein claimed that hell is not the other people, it is probably yourself. [I think hell is oneself among others.]

CLV

Reading through what some students have written about the very notion of interculturality I experience myself a 'meta-intercultural' shock. They speak of *cultural collision, integration* and *development*. I have a vague idea of what they mean but I am not *there* with them. Speaking about interculturality should always leave us in a state of interculturality: *We don't need to know, we don't need to understand, we don't need to convince and be convinced, we don't need to agree and... we don't need to think we are 'right'.*

CLVI

Interculturality is always a transition so I cannot 'snatch' it. Always in between, always in transition. *Transitionality*, always between *there is* and *there will be* – not opposition between them but them *together.*

CLVII

According to Alexander Blok (1880–1921) there is a difference in Russian between *kul'tura* (referring to *rootlessness, inauthenticity* – a term used by the 'elite') and *stikhiia* (*uncouth, elemental, unmediated* – a force that springs from the people). *You decide which one to apply to 'your' interculturality!*

Conclusions

This chapter is a tale of two discontents about what we know, what we prefer to know and what we decide to designate as knowledge. There is a difficulty in moving forward when a lot of voices clutch to the mainstream only, not to have any hesitations and doubts. The pleasure to know for a fact is unmatched and interculturality asks us to question and critique ourselves, otherwise, we would be stuck somewhere, taking pride in our misleading convictions. Interculturality may mean different things to the authors, which is reflected in the fragments, but they should be read in conjunction for the readers to be pushed, pulled and drawn towards various stances and knowledges. The readers can be learning and unlearning at the same time for the sake of developing their own situated knowledges rather than reading the authors for speaking their words later. The fragments feature a range of personal stories that reverberate numerous moments of reality mixed with some struggling to make sense of the intricacies lying ahead within interculturality. The fragments are intense and they are indeed flags for readers to take a step ahead and disrupt their comfort where they may be seeking (disguised) truths rather than hesitations and doubts. A major conclusion here is that knowing and interpreting are incessant as we are always coming to know but we never get hold of that plain and explicit truth, especially with regard to interculturality.

[Questions for readers]

- What fragments have *shaken* you?
- Do you often engage in self-critique? Is self-critique more bearable than 'other-critique'?
- Does reading this book encourage you to write your own fragments?
- Aren't we often all implicated in *illusions*, tending to believe what we know is inaccurate for the sake of our comfort?
- Do you feel that illusions are fundamental to our wellbeing as epistemic subjects?

[Main keywords]

Axiology: The philosophical study of values and things we value. This could be applied to interculturality and what things we seem to foreground in our analyses and what we hold to be valuable. Axiology is used in the book to refer to systems of thinking and valuing across societies, communities and individuals.

Cognitive dissonance: Our academic discourses spawn multiple existential crises that we may frame and create allusions that are fundamentally distant from reality. A lot of discourses need some reality check that we do not construct alternative realities where we fabricate issues and their supposed solutions. This sense of detachment lends to some questions around scholars' incessant promissory rhetorics that may be self-feeding and self-assuring rather than interventions into our social realities.

Culpabilization: Holding systems, structures and people accountable for some issues. The problem here is not the potential 'accusatory attitude' but rather the selective process of holding some parties responsible but not others. Culpabilization is soothing to some and it grants some assurance that one is innocent and benign.

Death of cultures: This represents a real dilemma for interculturality. One may ask if cultures die, then what would be the purpose of intercultural studies? Cultures may never die since as much as some scholars are distancing themselves from 'culture', there are others who are keen on centring everything that speaks of 'culture' and its derivatives. Yet, cultures may be on their deathbed.

Epistemic emancipation: Granting people the right to think for themselves without the fear of (a) being labelled unscientific and derivative, (b) retaliation when producing knowledge requires unsettling what is mainstream and taken-for-granted to open a space for alternative perspectives, and being dismissed based on the lack of proximity of these perspectives from the dominant and mainstream. The sustainable affordances of epistemic freedom are limited because they do not speak of the ramification of exercising freedom while epistemic emancipation calls for the abolition of epistemic shackles and any potential consequences for exercising freedom.

Essai…Erreur…: Signifies our incessant endeavours to get hold of interculturality. It denotes how the process of knowing is inherently bound by learning and unlearning in a continuous labour of refining and digging. The process of knowing is not linear and it should not be. Researching interculturality is itself an altering experience.

Exteriority of modernity: All knowledges, ontologies, ecologies and practices that are superficially included within the broader system. Moving from the 'exterior' to the 'interior' stipulates removing the very characteristics that signify the exterior including how they look, sound and think. The exterior is an object, not a subject.

Politics of enunciation: The range of factors, interests and conditions that influence and determine what one would be (un)willing to enunciate, how it is enunciated and how the enunciation is perceived, evaluated and judged.

Power as priori: This is a lens of analysis that centres power as the most fundamental element in interpreting and parsing social realities. Power itself is not exclusively drawn within structures and systems but also embedded within discourses that form our understandings of these social realities per se. That is, power does not only dictate human communication but also shapes our understanding of the various dynamics involved in locating and altering oneself among other selves as is the case in interculturality.

Untrusted Epistemologies: The range of knowledges, theories and perspectives whose epistemological capacity is doubted and, thus, untrusted to be drawn on as legitimate sources and ways of knowing. 'Trust' is political and its parameters are historical and overlapped with other dimensions beyond what is epistemic.

References

Byram, M. (1997). *Teaching and Assessing Intercultural Communicative Competence.* Bristol: Multilingual Matters.

Cooper, J., & Carlsmith, K. M. (2015). Cognitive dissonance. In *International Encyclopedia of the Social & Behavioral Sciences: Second Edition* (pp. 76–78). Elsevier Inc. DOI: 10.1016/B978-0-08-097086-8.24045-2.

Datta, R. (2018). Decolonizing both researcher and research and its effectiveness in Indigenous research. *Research Ethics*, 14(2), 1–24. DOI: 10.1177/1747016117733296.

Deleuze, G., & Guattari, F. (2017). Percept, affect and concept. In C. Cazeaux (Ed.), *The Continental Aesthetics Reader* (pp. 617–646). London: Routledge.

Mann, M. (1984). Capitalism and militarism. In M. Shaw, M. (Ed.), *War, State and Society* (pp. 25–46). London: Palgrave Macmillan.

Moussaid, M. (2021). *Fouloscopie: Ce que la foule dit de nous.* Paris: J'ai Lu.

Murdoch, I. (1977). *Interview with Bryan Magee.* London: BBC Television.

Queffelec, A. (2016). Au contact de la beauté. https://www.radiofrance.fr/franceculture/podcasts/a-voix-nue/au-contact-de-la-beaute-7662578

Raška, P. (2022). On epistemic dissonance: Contesting the transdisciplinary disaster risk reduction education, research, and practices. *Frontiers in Earth Science*, 9. DOI: 10.3389/feart.2021.818361.

R'boul, H. (2022). Researching the intercultural: solid/liquid interculturality in Moroccan-themed scholarship. *The Journal of North African Studies*, 27(3), 441–462. DOI: 10.1080/13629387.2020.1814750.

Wicklund, R. A., & Brehm, J. W. (1976). *Perspectives on Cognitive Dissonance.* Hillsdale, NJ: Erlbaum.

4 Further intuitions

Introduction

This last chapter relies on the idea of *intuitions* ('further intuitions') to share both meditation-like and forward-looking fragmentary pieces of writing concerning interculturality. The word *intuition* is from Latin for *a looking at, consideration*. It contains the idea of *watching over*, sharing the stem with words such as *a tutor* in English.

The intuitions to unfold represent both hypotheses and proposals to stimulate future engagement with the tricky notion that has interested us in this book. They urge us to 'sharpen' our thinking about it *endlessly*.

Five subsections compose the chapter: [Anaphoras], [Experiencing language ecstasy], [Adopting lateral thinking], [Validating and indulging in contradictions and opposite realities], [Shouldering thoughts backstage]. At the beginning of the chapter, in e.g. [Anaphoras] (repetitions of a word), mantra-like fragments containing metaphors, we reflect further *out loud* about the potential meanings, characteristics and uncertainties of interculturality. We then focus on the central issue of languaging around the notion again and again to support moving to and fro in just ways, taking into account diverse, 'beyond the West' and multilingual perspectives. *Lateral thinking* (thinking from 'the side') is proposed as a way of thinking 'beyond the box', focusing on the contradictions and opposite realities that interculturality forces us to experience and co-construct together. Lateral thinking calls for us to undo and redo ad infinitum what interculturality could be and entail. The chapter ends on more personal perspectives related to our own life experiences as scholars 'doing' interculturality in different parts of the world, reminding us of the importance and necessity to not ignore the influence of these aspects on our scholarship and knowledge (co-)construction.

[Anaphoras]

An anaphora is the repetition of a word at the beginning of successive sentences to produce specific effects (e.g., rhetorical and/or poetic). The following

DOI: 10.4324/9781003458050-4

anaphoric fragments urge us to think through the imperfect beauty of interculturality, the contradictions and insecurities that it triggers and reveals in us and
others, its *simplexities* (simplicity + complexity) as well as the impossibilities
of fully comprehending it. These anaphoras expose our inner thoughts, hypo-
thetical 'think aloud' reflections and struggles.

○

Interculturality is the 'limitless' of human encounters. It has no beginning,
no end. It started even before we see it happen in front of our eyes, ears and
minds. *It never really stops.* Every time I meet a new person, I meet other
people, ideas, ideologies, words, discourses, faces... Interculturality is always
embedded in the broader temporal and spatial even when I see it as a 'separate' bubble of encounters between you and me. We must thus reconsider the
nature of the boundaries we establish for interculturality.

一

    Interculturality is eternal.
    It morphs all the time.
    It has no beginning, no middle, no end.
    Treat it as everlasting.

二

Interculturality is a constantly co-constructed changing self-other-portrait.
    Interculturality is a *trompe l'oeil* [French for *deceiving the eye*]. It cannot
be otherwise...

三

Interculturality is unfinished in perpetuity. Interculturality triggers a zeigarnik
effect on us. We tend to remember things that are unfinished, we must come
back to interculturality again and again.
    [As an unfinished task, interculturality puts into question all models of
intercultural competence that lure us into believing that we can look at it in
the eyes and say: *I am done with you!*]

四

Interculturality is a chiliagon – a star polygon with 1,000 sides and 1,000
corners.

五

Interculturality is like pieces of mosaic that we throw on the table but cannot (and don't have to) recompose.

六

Interculturality is an acknowledgement of the complexities inherent in human communication and, thus, it does not draw a pink picture of social reality. Interculturality does not claim that it can solve issues or make the world a more peaceful place.

七

Interculturality is a plagiary of the simplexities [simplicities + complexities (Dervin, 2016)] of the world.

八

Interculturality is a long list of accidents. Without accidents, we are not facing the inevitable changes of life.

九

Interculturality is always in a position of equilibrium to survive, otherwise it is *something else*.

十

Interculturality is a field that studies the imbalanced. It reminds people of what they pretend (not) to know.

十一

Interculturality is a drama/comedy of verbal seesaw.
    [The seesaw as a metaphor for what we do together as intercultural 'doers'.]

十二

Interculturality is the study of inequalities and injustices.
    [As an eternal process of in-betweennesses, interculturality cannot befriend equalities or justices.]

十三

Interculturality is about what matters. You through me or myself through you and how inequalities shape who is the self and the other.

十四

Interculturality is relentless activating rather than (fully) indoctrinating.

十五

Interculturality is liberation rather than encasement.

十六

Interculturality is neither a job nor a task. *It just is.*

[Experiencing language ecstasy]

Language ecstasy is experienced when one is forced to think 'otherwise' about interculturality through the realization that meanings and connotations go beyond the expected and the taken-for-granted. Language ecstasy, which should be central in research and education, has to lead to a feeling of estrangement, of being an outsider in a conceptual world that appears to be 'normal'. It should lead us to 'taste' different ideological takes on interculturality, to which we do not necessarily have access when blinded by linguistic illusions of sameness and even 'could not care less' ("a word is a word"). In this subsection, we play with words; we play with the idea that words should disrupt scholars and educators involved with interculturality. When language 'remains'; when it is 'routinesque', 'empty' and 'obvious'; when language does not call out to us anymore as scholars, interculturality cannot but be frozen in time and space. The work of House and Kadar over the past years, where they examine the polysemy of concepts such as 'civilized' and 'nationalism' in Chinese and English, is fascinating here and deserves to be explored by interculturalists (e.g. Liu et al., 2021; House et al., 2022).

* Beyond trying to control and outwit interculturality? *

○

Ginseng taproots (growing vertically downward, see Figure 4.1) as a simplex symbol for languaging for interculturality. Dig out meanings, flavours and connotations from all directions!

[In Chinese, ginseng translates word for word as 'root of heaven'.]

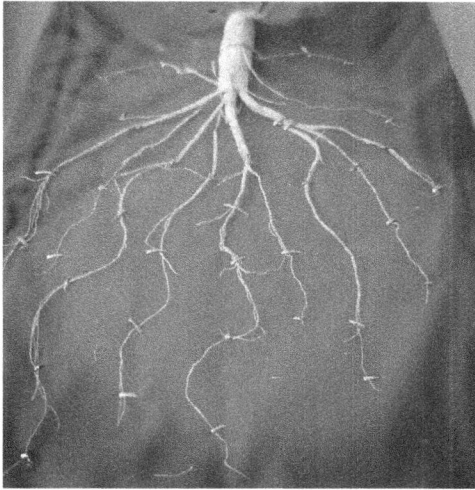

Figure 4.1 Ginseng taproots as a simplex symbol for languaging

一

In French, *connaissance – knowledge* – shares the same word as 'birth' (*naissance*). This is what interculturality is: re-birth through constant languaging rather than mere 'knowledge'.

二

An accent in someone's use of a language indicates the presence of at least two 'flavour worlds' for interculturality! *A minima* two ways of speaking about the notion; two ways of ideologizing it; two ways of dealing with it; two ways of re-constructing interculturality. The accent as a guarantee of *interculturalizing interculturality* (Dervin & Jacobsson, 2022).

三

Every discussion of interculturality must be multilingual because that's the only way it can be considered as a subject of research and education. Multilingualism within and between languages, dialects, sociolects... *My interculturality is definitely not always your interculturality* multilingually.

四

Finnish conductor Sakari Oramo (2020: n.p.) comparing Austrian composer and conductor Mahler's music (1860–1911) to e.g. the music of Finnish composer Jean Sibelius (1865–1957): "It's like a foreign language" – i.e. it disrupts the way people think about music. Interculturality must also be a 'foreign language' to the listeners, readers, speakers and interactants, providing them with a constant sense of estrangement to enrich their take on the notion.

[Music as a foreign language represents an interesting way to unthink and rethink how we mis-hear and mis-read sounds if we don't take the time to listen carefully. Like other 'types' of languages, learning so-called 'foreign' languages never guarantees being able to express oneself successfully. What they can do is make us rethink. We must treat interculturality like different languages that we need to study lifelong… we'll never speak them well enough. We must accept this fact.]

五

Marín-Arrese (2011: 789) drew attention to "the degree of commitment invoked in speakers'/writers' choice of epistemic stance expressions as legitimization strategies, as well as the expression of subjectivity/intersubjectivity in discourse and the degree to which this involves responsibility and accountability for the speaker/writer". This is not to absolve anyone but it certainly opens up possibilities for reimagining interepistemic dialogues. One can always rely on their privilege and/or their subalternity to legitimize what they argue for.

六

Metaphors are images. They are like sketches for art pieces. Let's use them more often for intercultural research and education instead of pretending to have reached a finished product.

七

The language of interculturality is a language in the making.

八

The very idea of 'European' *democratic culture* as a substitute for interculturality puts down the very notion by closing the door to the democratization of knowledges… Think carefully about the recycling of ideologies *engraved* in words: what is culture? What is democracy in the end? Who can say? Who can dictate to whom? Why should they?

九

Enlarge the boundaries of the permissible for engaging with intercultural research and education. Instead of *we should, we must*, let's try *we could, we might* and let's give it a try!

+

Our words will never outwit interculturality itself.

[Interculturality is too cunning. Interculturality can (easily) deflect our good intentions, manipulations, ideological orders in seconds.]

* Enriching our languaging of interculturality *

○

'Culture' is meaningful in 'intercultural communication' only if we expand its significance to include language, power and knowledge. We could move away from 'slogan words' in interculturality! (see Figure 4.2).

Figure 4.2 A so-called 'cultural shirt' in China, with the slogan-word *relativism* on its back

一

Vital thought: No language could ever describe interculturality. Interculturality occurs between you and me, thus in the in-betweenness of our relations, impressions, ideologies, manipulations... in the zigzagging of our thoughts.

二

We could fight against our own way of speaking about interculturality. Accept and name errors, imaginaries, dreams, ideologies...

三

We could develop new languages and dialects to talk about interculturality.

四

Develop your own language to talk about and deal with interculturality.

五

We could reinvent constantly our language to describe what we are trying to achieve for interculturality.

六

As much as we should reject the Western-centric word of *nature*, which denotes wobbly dichotomies (see Descola, 2013), maybe interculturality could be removed from our dictionaries and mouths. Let's try to create words that actually make sense for the simplexities of the human; words that change, words that exist to change, change to exist. Crystallizing words for interculturality is in fact closing the doors to both *inter-* and *-ity*, leaving many of us speaking for and over others.

七

Similarity in difference and difference in similarity. Today's anti-capitalism, anti-neo-liberalism, anti-neo-other-imposed-narcissism: China with the spread of the phrase *to lay flat* ('tang ping'); in the 'West': *quiet quitting* (Hsu, 2022).

八

Conversation in English with a Russian colleague about 'nationalities' during the Soviet times. He uses the words *nationalities* and *citizenship* in 'his' own ways (as much as I use them 'my' own ways). We try to understand each other but this requires long 'tasting' sessions. For him, it seems that the word *nationalities* is like *Minzu* in Chinese – i.e. it is about people who belong to different 'ethnic' groups (I use inverted commas since the word is treacherous in different Englishes and can mean many different things in different corners of the world). Considering the equation between the word 'nationalities' and what stands on 'passports' in e.g. the European Union, one can understand why mis-flavouring of these words can occur. More importantly, (moral) judgments can also emerge if conversations remain at the surface of each other's connotations (as in: 'they mistreat minorities' without understanding the local context). Speaking to my Russian colleague, I realized why it is that I have seen the word *nationalities* used in English to translate the word *Minzu* in China – which I refuse to translate today to avoid ideological 'miscalculations' (see Dervin & Yuan, 2021). The Chinese authorities did borrow at some point the stance of the Soviet authorities towards 'nationalities' and 'Minzu' (Xiaojun, 2017). The two words relate to interior affairs. Nationalities in 'Europe' is used to refer to relations, see 'confrontations', with the exterior.

Soviet Union/China	*'Europe'*
e.g. Kazakh (nationality/Minzu)	e.g. French
Chinese/Soviet (citizenship)	e.g. France

Dig into glocal flavours and archaeologies of interculturality!

九

Language is 'random' and yet manipulated and needs questioning in the way we name and feel things in its diverse forms. Take *October* as an example, the name for *month number 10*. Originally it referred to *month number 8* (*octovus* in Latin, see octopus). It became today's October after July and August were added in the *Roman* calendar. *Scrutinize any word used to discuss interculturality here and there, now and then!*

十

Listening to the thousands of diverse voices about interculturality found in all works of life is like putting one's head under water in the ocean where we can hear thousands of different sounds that we don't hear above water. Take the scallop (also known as e.g. *fan shell*) for example. These free-swimming invertebrates with up to 200 individual eyes along the edge of their mantle, produce a 'cough' sound when they move, clapping their shells quickly. Most of us will not have heard this sound. Working on interculturality urges us to listen to others' 'coughs' and to observe their 'invisible' eyes too…

十一

Reading perfume reviews, I cannot help but think about interculturality in different corners of the world. Someone sees in the same perfume *grey polished woods* and *black pepper*, another one, *pear, rose* and *pepper combination*.

十二

The English language has very few words for different kinds of smells and has borrowed from other senses to speak of them (e.g. *sweet, spicy*). We need more words for 'smelling' within interculturality discourses. For instance, the Jahai people from Malaysia are said to have a very specific word for the smell of *bat droppings* (Olofsson & Wilson, 2018). Whenever I come across a different perspective on interculturality, I need to develop specific and new vocabulary beyond my usual 'sense' to make sense of it and speak about it.

十三

There is a need in research on interculturality to coin 'metaphorical transfers' – i.e. following the etymology of metaphor: *to carry over, to bear across* – rather than 'scientific models', NB: *model* is from a Proto-Indo European root for *taking appropriate measures* (Kristeva, 2004: 28). What is appropriate for interculturality deserves to be debated again and again – and even banished!

十四

There are many homophones in Chinese (e.g. the characters for chopsticks also refer to six auspicious elements such as *happiness* and *quick birth of a child*). When we speak about interculturality, we should also check homophones. Interculturality has to be *homophonic* by nature.

十五

Beyond *achromatopsia* of interculturality? Beyond the absence of colour vision?

十六

Interculturality should be a riot of polysemy.

十七

Whatever could be said may have already been said, but whatever could be meant to be understood has not always been understood.

十八

There is a need to share our own silence in our writing on interculturality.

十九

Let silence speak.

二十

In music, the symbol of the rest denotes silence – the opposite of a note. Let's include rests in our writing on interculturality.

二十一

A *rahui* from Maori is a sign used to make a period of prohibition when e.g. a field is extra to consider resources. We could impose *rahui* on intercultural research. Be quiet for a while. Rest!

二十二

Extasis, the root of the word *ecstasy*, used to refer to *stepping back*. Let's experience that form of ecstasy in front of interculturality!

* Caring linguistically *

○

When I listen to others talking about interculturality, I must start listening to myself.

[This mirror effect is essential in 'practising' interculturality as both an object of research and education and a simplex phenomenon. Listening multi-directionally (inward included) should be a priority – *a caring priority*!]

一

Listening to someone requires to look at them in the eyes; hearing is more passive. At times, we hear someone in passing without looking at them, without caring to care.

二

I do not particularly enjoy reading what seems to be mannered and forced. It is unfortunate to acknowledge how we read what we want but we hardly ever write what we want. The very moment we start writing those marvellous ideas, we tarnish, distort and misrepresent them. Words often fall short in conveying our fragmented reasoning.

[Fred is tempted to write that this is the beauty of humanness. *We fail.* Many would consider this argument to be 'depressing', 'unappealing' and/or 'negative' having been fed with neoliberal ideologies of positivity and happiness. However, we all know this 'truth' of humanness too well. It is central in interculturality. Caring linguistically for and with interculturality thus requires accepting our tendencies to fail in the way we communicate.]

三

Stop using the reader as an excuse to justify your own ideological orders and agendas for interculturality.

四

Writing for others is an intercultural practice in which meanings are negotiated. It is often a one-way intercultural process when writing but it evolves into an ontological exercise of distancing oneself from situated perspectives to open up while reading the other.

[Speak to and with your readers! Write to and with your listeners!]

五

Writing can be overwhelming when the words do not match and/or reflect thoughts. The craft of turning abstracts into concretes carries a substantial level of risk in either distorting the essence of what is being thought of or ultimately delivering what cannot be accurately understood by others in ways that are faithful to the writer's imaginations and logics. This lends the question of whether interculturality can intervene in this morass of writing and reading. *Do we all read in the same way or does our ontological infrastructure shape our receptive lenses?*

六

We should start all our books, articles and talks about interculturality by reminding readers and listeners that one cannot write and/or talk about interculturality without stereotyping it, reducing it to what it could never be. Words will *always* make it too simple and crude in front of its complexities. Words disturb the *plasticity* of interculturality (from Greek *plastikos* for being able to be moulded into different shapes).

七

We should put words in sentences to personalize what these words mean. Interculturality as an isolated word is *meaningless*.

八

Words are treacherous and misleading. One does their best to convey their thoughts because one is preoccupied with the burden of sharing with others. *They are hoping that they can confront their thoughts and seep into them as they seep into their souls.* One can stand in front of those words and wonder who is using the other and who is at the mercy of the other. Humans are not words but words can always convince others that they represent human suffering and misery. The word 'motherhood' was probably invented by a man who used this very notion to appropriate whatever mothers feel. If something is describable, then it is under control; it is mundane and conceivable.

九

Repeat after me: "I shall not use the words *migrant-background* and *diversity* in my work without clarifying *a minima* who it is that I am targeting in my research and why I wish to 'speak' for and over them!" As I read these words you force me to imagine them – fair enough – but I am not sure if the fruit of my imagination is the same as yours – or why I should imagine them following your own ways. We need to be genuine so our minds can meet *a minima*.

十

There is no need to insert foreign words [i.e. words from other languages; but what is foreign in such a global language as English?] in English to talk about interculturality, to open it up when they are merely used to confirm what we (already) think we know. Opening the origami of languages should disrupt our thinking – not confirm it. Raking through the history books they represent should switch on new (temporary) lights. When I see newness in a word in any of the languages that I know, I am ecstatic. I want to see through different tunnels.

[The pleasure of discovering that the English word *Orientalism* found on a product package at a museum store in China is accompanied by a translation in Chinese that has nothing to do with e.g. Said's (1972) orientalism. 完美不必无缺 translates as 'perfection with flaws'. The package contained a copy of a broken piece of oracle bone where Chinese characters were first carved before paper was invented. Orientalism here stands for appreciating things that are not perfect, that deserve second chances. The notion in its Chinese 'flavours' is very much reminiscent of Kintsugi (literally *golden joinery*), the Japanese art of repairing broken pottery with gold.]

十一

In Venice in the Middle Ages, there was a special inn for German tourists called *Zu der Flöte* where one could only speak German dialects. A dog who was sitting there barked at anyone who did not speak it, urging them to use the language. As far as interculturality is concerned, we would need dogs barking at us every time we spoke *interculturalese* – this language that fakes being about interculturality but is in fact a limited, broken and often empty language rehearsing accepted ('Western') banalities.

十二

We should aim for onomatopoeic interculturality, sounding similar to the multiple and varied noises that we hear around the notion.

十三

Interculturalizing interculturality (Dervin, 2021) is the *democratization* of intercultural knowledge. That's the only use of the treacherous word of *democracy* that I can bear.

十四

We cannot just be 'devices' for interculturality – a word which etymologically has to do with dividing (from Latin divider *to divide*). As a device for very specific perspective on interculturality (e.g. democratic culture), I lead to divisions scientifically and educationally [and in the end economic-politically!]. What we need in times of emergencies like now is to 'unite' by opening up, being silent (at times) and observing.

十五

I appreciate when a scholar does not rely on their past achievements and reputation to simply say whatever. It is laudable when one is willing to listen to others and genuinely believes that others can say something as well.

十六

Like all words, interculturality can save us or kill us. *Care for yourself and others!*

[Adopting lateral thinking]

○

Step outside the machine of interculturality.

[Increasingly I consider research and education related to anything interculturality as *a machine* that seems to be made to work by itself. Stop the engine as often as you can and rest.]

一

We must all experience migration when dealing with interculturality – seeing it with new eyes!

[This fragment assumes that migrating means seeing with new eyes. But is it always the case?]

二

Giorgio Morandi's art is very much inspiring for un- and re-thinking interculturality. Throughout his career, he painted and engraved groups of objects (vases, bottles, distinctive shapes) and landscapes. These were the only and recurring characters of his art. Morandi (1890–1964) asks us to rethink and unthink what is behind these objects that looks so familiar by their recurrence. He also urges us to observe the tension between stillness and implied movement that he depicts through simple and yet complex lines and colours. It is the known, the unknown, the repeated and yet the new. His art plays with our anticipation and perception, just like interculturality.

What Morandi did with his art for several decades, we must do the same with interculturality: we re-present (present again!) it in as many diverse ways as we can.

三

Wang Wei (701–761 B.C.E.) wrote poetry and painted. He used the same brush for both activities. When we see his paintings, we hear his poetry; when we listen to his poetry, we can fell his art and observe landscapes. I have often felt that interculturality is the same: what we write about should as organic, lively and tangible as interculturality itself. [Could we ever reproduce/represent such characteristics in writing?]

四

More radical imagination would consist in asking how interculturality would be like if Africa was the actual Europe and Anglo-sphere, and brown/black supremacy was the norm. These are very fascinating worlds to think about. Modernity would be defined by the mainstream ontologies of e.g. Morocco, Algeria and Tunisia. The highest-ranking universities would be in e.g. Kenya, Mali and Cameroon. To ostensibly receive the best possible education that would significantly propel one's job prospects and epistemic capacity, one would need to spend some time in Africa. The underlying assumption would be if one was accepted and endorsed by Africa, they would be welcomed and positively perceived everywhere. International talents will be seeking opportunities in Africa. Internationalization would be the Africanization of institutions, frameworks, policies and people. Africa would be selective in receiving immigrants and impose stringent visa requirements on people coming from the Global North (which is the Global South in this imagination). The Global North would be grateful for the African colonization of Europe and the Anglo-sphere because they had built roads, institutions and airports. Decolonization would mean the de-Africanization of all spheres of existence.

五.

What interculturality would sound and look like if the leading scholars in the field were from Africa and working at African universities? International students from Finland and Spain would be earnestly trying to be affiliated with African universities because they would be aware that once they decided to go back, they would be valued over the other students who had studied in their own countries since the local education and expertise is deemed inferior and of way less quality. Acculturation would mean that Finnish and Spanish immigrants would be abstracting away from their original cultural conceptions and embracing African knowledges, perspectives and ontologies because they are more modern and attractive. The supranational institutions that exert a massive impact on how interculturality is theorized and exercised would be founded upon African 'ethics and 'values'. Scholars would need to look and sound African to have their epistemic capacity reaffirmed and to be, thus, included in the circles that steer the wheel of interculturality research and education.

六

Interculturality pushes us to play hide and seek with each other – *the notion and us, that is!*

七

The obvious, the politically disguised as cultural, racial, ethnic, etc., the fake in research on interculturality. These are my 'competitors'.

八

Not democracy, not social justice, not human rights, but a responsibility to take interculturality seriously, to treat it in all its complexities.

九

My political stance is to uncover and unveil politics in intercultural communication education and research.

十

Genealogies of thought are important in fathoming the very epistemic essence of some theories. Why, how and what for are essential questions to develop well-rounded understandings of the perspectives we are engaging with.

[We might want to add the word *ideologies* (orders, hidden agendas, manipulations of thoughts, Roucek, 1944) to the loose and 'friendly' word of *perspectives*.]

十一

Stop hiding behind so-called theories! This 'solid' Western-centric word (from Greek) is used as a protection today as if one were saying: "I am strong; I have a weapon called *theory* which makes me undefeatable". *The only theory we need for interculturality is* change – *thus the hyphen between self and the other, the balancing of self and other*. A theory must promote change at the core of interculturality.

十二

The thing about concepts is not so much about how we understand them but more about why we feel we should make use of them.

十三

In order to deal with interculturality, we must be experts in destroying concepts, 'ideas', words.

十四

Philosophy is fundamentally essential for interculturality theorizings and analyses.
[What philosophy means and aims to is polysemic in different corners of the world (Abdul-Jabbar, 2022; Bateye et al., 2023). Yet, one thing that

different philosophies seem to share is that they push us to think further and to consider questions – realizing that answers are not necessarily needed, can be delayed or explored again and again. What could be more inspiring for interculturality? I have 'practised' philosophy as a student and an amateur for over 30 years, shifting and navigating in the past decade from 'our' Western philosophy to other philosophies.]

十五

Observe the way an idea is bearing changes. How it is altered in you, with and through others.

十六

Research has to be honest, direct and loyal to reality not construct imaginations that sugar-coat the world's inequalities, injustices and misfortunes.

十七

Interculturality urges us to adopt *pain feng* – a term in Chinese calligraphy referring to a brush stroke to the side. To think laterally and creatively, to not follow trends and the taken-for-granted.

[This could potentially serve as an explanation for the idea of 'doing' and 'thinking' interculturality *otherwise*, which we have both discussed. Twist ideas, words, concepts, methods to the side in order to explore new aspects of the notion. Whenever one thinks that something is 'obvious' or 'straightforward', *pain feng!*]

十八

The only skill needed for becoming a researcher of interculturality is *synesthesia*: seeing colours where we hear sounds, and vice versa.

十九

Like art, interculturality is always changing because it relies on the eyes, ears and mouth of the beholder. Let them see, hear, feel whatever they want.

二十

Interculturality needs to be politicized. This stipulates that scholars centre socio-political issues in their narratives and discourses.

二十一

Like art, research on interculturality must be transgression. Let things fly towards the impermissible! *That's freedom.*

二十二

We must sabotage and mistreat language when we write about interculturality. Language is a prison whose gates we must break open. Language forces us to speak in certain ways about interculturality. *It silences us in the process. It silences our complexities.* Language is too strong, too static, too imprisoning to express, construct interculturality in its fluidity. We must thus shake it; we must lead a revolution against language; we must break it loose! Invent new words, twist the old ones, borrow other words. Confront words in different languages. Make language as fluid and contradictory as interculturality!

二十三

When I write scholarly texts about interculturality I must write for those whom I imagine will
disagree with me – not those who will follow my ideological wor(l)ds blindly.

二十四

Abandon your *libido dominandi* (*desire to dominate*) in research and education for interculturality. Just surrender and let others disagree.

二十五

Scholars in interculturality need to start thinking against themselves. A lot of assumptions are situated within Europe and then extended to other peripheries. Being intercultural means being interested not only in where benefits can be made, e.g., Asia and the Middle East, but also in the peripheries and disadvantaged spaces, e.g., Africa.

二十六

Have the courage to systematically disagree interculturally.

二十七

This unapologetic disposition to reclaim the legitimacy of apolitical perspectives and notions in interculturality despite the renewed urge to consult epistemologies born in struggle belies the very attempts to undo benevolent and pink drawings of interculturality through numerous calls. It is amazing how the long-continued imports of competence, citizenship and skills in interculturality and intercultural education still bear repeating despite the previous vehement critique. They supply the understanding that humans are inherently good, and with a bit of education and training, they would be more inclined to sustain equitable and mutually-satisfying communicative and interactive ontological practices.

二十八

Our duty is to know more about different ways of dealing with interculturality. The more we know the readier we are to change the way we engage with the notion. This is in fact the most important aspect of ethics in intercultural research and education.

二十九

I encourage early-career scholars to seek independence. It is understandable that working with seniors may allow one to have multiple publications, but it is also important to strike a balance in order not to be referred to as 'someone's student'. Also, senior scholars could normalize disagreement and critique in the sense that early career scholars have no issue pinpointing elements to be challenged and questioned.

三十

We should not be mere epigones, followers and disciplines, especially inferior imitators of powerful (and yet necessarily imperfect) voices in intercultural education and research.

三十一

It is essential that interculturality theory expands its horizons to examine other under-researched areas. It is overly obsessed with intersubjectivity and humans with this fantasy for rationalizing culture as the priori for explaining behaviours, thoughts and perspectives.

三十二

Any systemic analysis of power relations within interculturality has to probe into how much interculturality exists within the interculturality field. The problematic is the answer may be unclear since the field may not reflect what it preaches. This contradiction poses an adamant epistemological dilemma in the field and how it genuinely researches and addresses what it purports to.

三十三

South-South relations and dynamicity are interesting topics to be researched more seriously within interculturality (R'boul et al., 2023). For instance, a lot of Moroccan students are increasingly opting for their higher education studies in China. Also, a substantial number of sub-Saharan students are coming to continue their studies in Morocco. The parameters of these encounters are considerably dissimilar to the usual factors considered within our analyses of interculturality. Studies in intercultural communication have concentrated on Southern individuals in the Global North but they have little to say about South-South interculturality and acculturation. This is a line of inquiry that carries fundamental intricacy that requires epistemological nuance and depth in which linguistic, cultural and epistemic hierarchies sustain great relevance. This line of inquiry would probably be granted more convergence and importance in future research on interculturality. I hope that this topic would be researched through Southern lenses because they would have real-life experiences and more grounded insights into these relations and dynamics.

三十四

South-South dialogue is a captivating case of interculturality because its dynamicity is conditioned by factors that may be alien to the dominant discourses in intercultural communication (R'boul, 2023). The focus of decolonial and postcolonial theories is always on North-South relations as the only possible direction of human communication.

三十五

There are some irregular and unusual flows of interculturality that are unexamined and unexplored terrains of interculturality. For example, a Moroccan in Mexico, a Chinese in Congo, a Brazilian in Taiwan and an Egyptian in the Dominican Republic; these encounters have some great potential in invalidating some dominant theories around interculturality and renewing the field to consider some dimensions and dynamics that have never been approached before.

三十六

Whenever social activism is discussed and sought, it is essential to emphasize the locality of knowledge. The available literature provides remarkable insights, but it is important, in order to ensure the effectiveness of educational policies and praxis, to align any theory to the very context where intervention is needed.

三十七

Students need to be assisted in navigating the literature. Scholars need years of experience to be able to draft a compelling literature review. Early-career scholars do not develop in linear ways dictated by their intelligence but rather by how much assistance and guidance they have received or the lack of it. [Beyond 'guiding', the only way to learn to 'navigate' the literature is by developing interdisciplinary curiosity, *reading, reading, reading, reading, reading, reading...* Dialoguing with one's reading is the best form of intellectual training.]

三十八

It is necessary that we study interculturality within history because it may illuminate the grounds upon which hierarchies have been based and from which they have derived their adamancy and legitimacy.

三十九

In recent years, there have been vehement calls for more justice with varying levels of analysis of inequalities. It is absolutely necessary to foreground contemporary solidarity struggles between distinct social movements to exert more impact.

四十一

I see interculturality as a field of inquiry where power is the most fundamental element for capturing how intercultural encounters have been unfolding.

[Although power has become some kind of a 'must' in intercultural research (and, increasingly, a 'soft' claim), it is often used to examine and 'criticise' *some* research participants and/or attack those researchers who disregard and somehow contribute to power imbalances. However, we are all *power abusers*. We need to see and be placed in front of our own abuses so we can act upon them. Any utterance about interculturality in research and education is somehow an act of power imbalance.]

四十二

Interculturality should not be an ideological tool for the dominants only but a range of tools for all ideologies to flourish and take centre stage (in turn). *Enrich our ideological worlds!*

四十三

We need to abstract away from these flat analyses that foreground one axe of power and not others. Individuals' lived experiences are founded upon complex dynamics of intersectionalities depending on time and/or space. It is crucial that any analysis of power asymmetries and interculturality is deeply grounded in temporal intersectionality that is in play through and among people in that specific time and space.

四十四

Interculturality may be within metaphysics. It draws on a substantial number of assumptions that draw a picture of human relations to be 'there' and ready for us to apply our theories to unravel and analyse its dynamics. Interculturality seems to encompass several deliquescent elements that entail the same level of epistemological wandering in such as happiness, the purpose of life and ontology.

四十五

It is interesting to examine interculturality in relation to *comfort*. Some people may have a natural inclination to navigate intercultural encounters stress-free, while for others they could be experiences filled with anxiety even if they are scholars of interculturality.

四十六

Interculturality as an object of research and education could be mimetic of what people experience not fantasies of what they should experience.

四十七

No need to try to mutilate interculturality further in research and education. Just let her become.

四十八

Any theoretical approach to non-Western art should seek to undermine the narratives and the understandings that assimilate southern creativities into the logics of Western artistic theory.

四十九

Because creative practices are not only shaped by culture (Hondzel & Gulliksen, 2015; Shao et al. 2019) but are also modes of cultural representations, an important aspect of the relationship between creativity and interculturality is how different creative ontologies are shared, exchanged and made sense of. In the ontological sense, there is an inaccuracy in presenting creativity in a singular connotation assuming artistic alignment and homogeneity of innovative visions. The diversity of cultural formations implies the existence of multiple 'creativities' underpinned by different perceptions of what constitutes aesthetic value, artistic ingenuity and originality; an assumption that renders any context of artistic consumption at the international level a space where various creative ontologies interact in intercultural dynamics.

五十

Creativity is fundamentally interrelated with culture in dyadic dynamics as it produces products, images and ideas that are valued and understood differently within different cultural contexts, to be appreciated, embraced, cultivated, or rejected. These assumptions emphasize not only the presence of "contrasting conceptions of creativity across cultures", but also "the role of the cultural context in the development, expression, and assessment of creativity" (Mourgues et al., 2015, p. 255). Interpreting works of art is necessarily a part of the artistic analysis which should not be conducted through prescribed theoretical frameworks that are largely fixed or not informed by any cultural orientation. It is useful to consider that arts are, in a way, artistic markers of cultures. Due to the unsystematic/nonlinear state of artistic production, communication of creativities is ideally expected to deny any understanding that presents "creativity as an essentialist and objectively measurable reality" (Hocking, 2018).

五十一

Arts, film, music, theatre and clothing create human interaction and generate a form of communication that is mostly abstract and can be abstruse/esoteric. People from different contexts or cultures have distinct perspectives on the inherent meaning of creativity, art and aesthetics. Therefore, creativity may be communicated through culture-related frames in some cases, but communication is accurate only when culturally appropriate rubrics are used. Interpreting creative outputs from different cultures is again largely dependent on the nature of interpretation. Different individuals may generate different understandings of a particular work because of not only their various frames of mind but also the type of analysis and interpretation that someone has relied on to conceive an artwork. Creativities may receive contrasting appraisals depending on who the receiver is and how extensive their artistic knowledge is.

五十二

Situating these hegemonic narratives of modernity and coloniality of power, knowledge and being (Quijano, 2000, 2007; Maldonado-Torres, 2007) within the global discussion of artworks would identify similar restrictions and contradictions that emanate from the geopolitics of knowledge (Mignolo, 2018). The underlying tendency in these colonial-like processes, which often get normalized and hidden by the narrative of modernity, is to silence or discredit "the historical specificity and productivity of postcolonial narratives and genealogies in artistic practices and cultural forms, a crucial and paralyzing elision" (McCarthy & Dimitriadis, 2000, p. 59). Reformulating the very processes and biases involved in knowledge production about artworks is necessary to transcend colonialist, monocultural frames in communicating creativities. The aim is to give rise to non-derivative thinking developed from unlearning Northern-Western epistemologies and creativities and anchored in the cultural and social fabric of the global south.

五十三

I think authors' geopolitical locations need be taken into account when critically reading and/or reviewing works. It does not sound reasonable to assess two works authored by people conditioned by substantially dissimilar conditions, frameworks and understandings, in the same way, drawing on the same (reading) grid.

五十四

Drawing on decoloniality can help realize an alternative definition of interculturality.

五十五

By the end of the day, what others have to say about interculturality should not necessarily be our main focus – they might be lying or merely parroting what they have been taught and told to believe in, without even really caring about what they are uttering. What is interesting is to use what they say as a mirror to look into our own *interculturalscapes* and discourses.

五十六

Loss of meaning: many words mean nothing or everything at the same time. *Juggle with words in all directions when dealing with interculturality.*

五十七

Towards the evocation of interculturality versus its description.

五十八

Unconventional should be the keyword for research on interculturality. *Stop rehearsing!*

五十九

As someone working on interculturality, I must tune my seismograph – feeling the movements of all things in the balancing acts that the notion represents.

六十

We should always consider interculturality under the lens of people who will never get to meet each other – not just through the (often fantasized) lens of those who do meet.

六十一

In interculturality I must consider self, other and the more-than-human as *the double*, like shadows, images reflecting on water, looks in the mirror, twins…

六十二

It is important that readers have a 'good' impression of you as a human and scholar in order for them to make efforts to understand you.

六十三

To create inspiration in the way we deal with interculturality in research and education we could adopt the process of counter-illumination that a squid experiences when they swallow certain types of bacteria. They start 'shining' after ingurgitating them. We must 'counter-illuminate' our thoughts through other takes on the notion.

六十四

Bear seeing yourself in the mirror of interculturality of the other! At times, remember to pinch yourself to come back to your realities!

六十五

Why is it that when one dialogues directly with one's readers in a book, one's writing is then considered as 'textbook-like'? Isn't any writing about *relating to others*? Write outside the sphere of 'academic' monologism! Ignoring the 'ears' lent to us is negating the very processes of interculturality that we write about – thus 'low quality' intercultural scholarship.

六十六

It is not about explaining but helping oneself and others feel.

六十七

My works seek to construct a different landscape upon which alternative epistemic and intellectual movements are articulated.

六十八

With all these pushes to freely choose one's gender identity, I wonder why we don't do the same with interculturality? *Today I am Japanese, Brazilian and Italian. Today I am raceless. Today, I am a human.*

六十九

Everyone and everything is transcendable including those ideas and theories that have been foundational in our understanding of intercultural relations. It is important to destruct to build later or at least disrupt what has been dominant but less relevant to others.

七十

Malleability is the keyword for working on interculturality.

七十一

It takes a lot of self-confidence to be creative in research on interculturality.
    [And yet it is vital.]

[Validating and indulging in contradictions and opposite realities]

The intuitions presented in this section could be considered in fact *counterintuitive* since they urge us to look at interculturality through the lenses of contradictions and opposite realities. As a simplex phenomenon that pushes us in all directions (rather than putting us 'on track') interculturality should be considered in research and education by focusing on these central aspects of what it might be and entail. We propose to 'indulge' in them as a way of continuously enriching our takes on the notion.

○

The only proper approach to interculturality is the one that contradicts itself appropriately.

一

Challenge yourself once a day. Identify an idea, a concept you dis-/like about interculturality. Undo and redo them. Create new words to refer to the phenomena they describe. Shake off automatons that have been passed onto you. *Can you feel the difference? Can you re-live interculturality human-like? Are you human again?* Continue. Don't stop.

二

I don't study interculturality. Interculturality studies me.

三

Any view on interculturality as an object of research and education could be an anamorphosis, i.e. a perspective technique providing a changing un-/distorted image of a subject depending on how one looks at it.

四

Say goodbye to the grandeur of ideas. *Smaller ideas wanted!*

五

A nice phrase from Serbian *zubato sunce* refers to the sun in winter – it looks hot but very cold outside. It means literally *the sun with big teeth*. Interculturality as an object of research and education often gives us the same impression.

六

Argue against the need to choose *between*!

七

We need intercultural coincidences, accidents to escape from our beliefs, ide-ologies and own tastes.

八

Des-alienize interculturality while feeling alien to it!

[Interculturality cannot be paused beyond the balancing processes of *I-it-us-them.*]

九

While we think that we make interculturality through research and education, interculturality makes us, often *underground.*

十

Disagree. Disagree with others. Disagree with yourself. Disagree with the past, the present, the future. *Just disagree, and especially agree to differ!*

To agree is from old French *agreer* for *to please, satisfy; to receive with favour, take pleasure in.* Interculturality should never be about pleasing or satisfying but about 'interring'…

十一

Humans are not intercultural beings by definition. Whatever the intercul-tural could mean, it remains questionable to what extent interculturality is an innate state of being where people build, shape and mould their mind-sets and identities in ways that make sense to them. Philosophy has always stressed the importance of the other in understating oneself as a mirror from which perceptions of ourselves are constructed. However, this mirror also generates assumptions around superiority/inferiority. The mirror is not be-nign or neutral; it is subjective and power-laden. The mirror has its own opinions that are reverberated and conveyed to people. Humans are national and tribal beings who would always grant superiority to their own groups.

[We are both victims and perpetuators of all kinds of -isms. Trying to break off from them is a cul-de-sac. We can barely pretend to do so.]

十二

To think interculturally is to liberate ourselves from interculturality.

[Interculturality is not (obviously) one but many. Liberating ourselves from *the one* is a necessity.]

十三

To make people talk about interculturality, ask them to share what it is not about or what they don't like about what others say about it.

十四

What I think interculturality is and entails should remain *mine* – and mine only! It should not be followed by the thousands of researchers and educators who work on the notion in every corner of the world. [Break away from trends to liberate our balancing acts.]

十五

Our usual behaviours and practices that are thought to be casual, normal and spontaneous are incredibly ideological and biased. A lot of racist, discriminatory and supremacist acts are often unintended. Interculturality needs to dig deeper into our inadvertent actions that exude an unconscious, or unacknowledged, sense of superiority over others. However, this also relates to our unwitting sense of inferiority which has been normalized through the long-continued ages of marginality.

十六

One can never approach interculturality in a state of 'virgin maidenhood'. All previous encounters count towards deflowering.

十七

Interculturality is bound to devour itself!

十八

Conflicts about interculturality can allow us to identify false beliefs and contest our ideological assumptions.

十九

Glimpse beyond the veil of interculturality. See snapshots of its simplex realities but never imagine staring at it in the eyes.

二十

Culture is an effective mechanism for rationalizing superiority and/or inferiority.

二十一

Contradictions by nature must contradict themselves.
[*Ad infinitum*]

二十二

Let's X-ray any idea related to interculturality to unearth its depths and contradictions.

二十三

Intercultural, too intercultural – *No choice.*

二十四

People (don't) know how to 'do' interculturality together. Let them do it the way they want to *with others*. Let them fail *with others*. Let them develop their own style *with others*. Let them change *with others*.
[Let interculturality be! Control.]

二十五

Interculturality must be a mirror of transformation – not imitation.

二十六

Leave space to other legibilities. *Grasp, apprehend and comprehend them!*

二十七

Interculturality should be treated *abruptly* – an adverb from Latin *abruptus* for broken off, precipitous, steep and disconnected. All the characteristics of interculturality!

二十八

Interculturality as *zeugma* (from Greek, *a boat bridge*) – one word made to refer to two or more nouns in a sentence but applying only to one. *Two opposed worlds bridged? But who wins? Or is there a winner?*

[Winning/losing are central in interculturality. Although unvoiced, these phenomena should be countered.

Is the metaphor of the bridge improper unless we remain on the bridge together and do not cross over?]

二十九

We must rebel against dominating ideologies. We must rebel.

[While reviewing this fragment, I am reminded that a 'discarded' ideology (if that is even possible) will always be replaced by another ideology. Rebelling must be multi-dimensional and -directional.]

三十

During a body massage, I shift from crying, smiling, laughing, screaming. I am thinking of the work I do on interculturality. The masseur helps my body to be reborn, like some of my co-authors, some of those I read, some of the music I listen to, some of the art I see, some of the observations I make on a daily basis. *Life as a massage for interculturality.*

三十一

Interculturally speaking, revise what we think is unjust-natural, essentialist-logical and imaginary-real.

[Revise our (un-)necessary dichotomies!]

三十二

The word *naïve* comes from Latin *natius* for *not artificial*. Let's be more naïve about interculturality!

三十三

Interculturality is never an option.

[The word *option* might come from a Proto-Indo European root for *to choose, to grab* and comes from old French for having the power or liberty to choose. Since interculturality relies on constant balancing of self and other (Tian & Dervin, 2023), it is highly unrealistic to believe in 'choosing' or 'grabbing'.]

三十四

We must be narcissistic in intercultural research and education! We must look at ourselves, listen to ourselves, accept that our views and ideas are also worth sharing – not just stare at those who have the power to tell us what interculturality is about and what it should entail. *This era is over.*

[Narcissism is often seen as a 'bad' thing. However, staring at self – especially in reaction to staring at the other – could help us change and expand our views on interculturality.]

三十五

Deciding what not to do with interculturality is as imperative as planning what to do with and through it.

三十六

Change happens all the time in interculturality. These co-constructions/negotiations always lead to experiencing contradictions in us and the other.

三十七

The majority of the most renowned literature is about pain, struggle and misery rather than happiness, love and peace.

[Cut off from neoliberal thoughts of *enrichment!*]

三十八

Interculturality does not teach how to interculturalize. Interculturality problematizes and constructs profound understandings of intercultural relations that for some may seem far away from reality.

三十九

Getting rid of our pre-structures is goal number one for interculturality.

四十一

Although it is often claimed that we are divided ideologically between the 'West' and the rest, the current global search and obsession for 'happiness' is a clear ideological agenda that we are all forced to worship!

四十二

Chinese reversible (Huiwenshi) poems as a metaphor for working on interculturality. A text usually has a beginning (e.g. use of opening quotes and a capital letter) and an end (marked e.g. by the use of a full point). *Huiwenshi* creates endless meanings by giving the opportunity to readers to read poems in any direction, i.e. one can choose any 'entry word' in the poem and read in any direction. Some Huiwenshis appear in the form of circular poems that can be read horizontally, vertically, diagonically and spiral-like. A real labyrinth of thoughts – like interculturality.

We must turn and hurl interculturality in all directions.

四十三

"I'm sure you all agree with me. Interculturality requires…". *The end of dialogue*. Systematically disagree.

[Do we need consensus? Do we need agreements? Aren't these phenomena 'castrating' the inter-? Aren't they often mere performances since the powerful figure (an often unstably established one) will always win? Accept winning AND losing!]

四十四

Interculturality has never been, is not and will never be *a theory*. Only if theory is considered through its ancestor from Greek theōros ('spectator'), then it might guide us to observe what we do to it, with it, for it, instead of it, especially together with others.

四十五

Fragmentation is an accurate and faithful representation of our ideas about interculturality; the field is diverse and increasingly divergent but there seems to be a disinclination to unlearn those ready-made simplistic understandings of the intercultural.

[Fragmentation as a natural synonym for interculturality (Dervin, 2022).]

四十六

You don't have to win at interculturality. It is neither ping pong nor tennis between us. Ideally, we just continue 'playing'.

四十七

We have to accept that interculturality cannot but lead us to treason. We are all 'traitors'.

四十八

Interrelatedness between individuals as transformative foundations.

[Transformation as a simplex phenomenon that can hardly be grasped by the one who experiences it and their observers.]

四十九

Our continuous critiques of culture and its usage as a priory to explain certain perspectives and behaviours may create this stigma of actually trying to understand phenomena through culture. As much as I alert readers to the importance of eschewing 'culture' as an index and marker, there is a wide range of things within a culture that are quite influential. We cannot simply deny culture for the sake of sounding anti-essentialist. Culture (regardless of how it is defined) is always there within and through us but it may materialize through varying degrees and shapes.

五十

There is already epistemic asymmetry in conversation (Sidnell, 2012) which is adamant; whatever is said is sometimes assessed by drawing on one's status.

五十一

Subalternizing others is not a characteristic of a specific group of people; it is a feature of the human race.

五十二

It is essential to encourage a perspective of interculturality that does not assume that intercultural encounters are benign, benevolent and equal. Interculturality is political, and it is something else if it is not concerned with sociopolitical issues of human communication.

五十三

Social realities are various, plural and entangled. That is, they do not have to go through the same analytical lenses but rather through epistemic trajectories that centre conditions, circumstances and ecologies.

五十四

Recycling of subalternity could be a human characteristic. We are as good, benevolent and ethical as our abilities and power allow us to be. As soon as those who are marginalized are in a position of power with regard to others, they may exercise the same sense of superiority against those who come next down in the hierarchy.

五十五

Hospitality and inclusion for all must start from knowledge about interculturality – while trying to lower signs of hierarchy. *Hospitality and inclusion are intrinsically about power relations.*

五十六

South-South interculturality is a genuine case of power asymmetries. One can expect that peripheries would lead to a collective subjectivity by which they could confront geopolitical challenges, but they again choose to situate people under labels, boxes and hierarchies.

五十七

It is quite hard to be continuously self-conscious about the process of emulating other prominent scholars whose influence on oneself is significant. Writing the actual manuscript with a scholar one has been looking up to is more intense and challenging.

五十八

Working on interculturality we should toil through it with the principle of *Gesamt Kunstwerk* in mind: *mixed-media, science, art, music, performance…* not just 'political ideas' disguised as research ideas. Interculturality as a broader notion (ideological construct?) than the ideologically limited.

五十九

Interculturality is more nuanced and effective when it is about complexity in understanding lived experiences rather than describing intersubjective processes.

六十

It makes no sense to preach about interculturality when one is entirely encapsulated in one's own epistemic circles. Interculturality is about cross-fertilization and having one's logics shaped by various epistemologies.

六十一

The only way to liberate and emancipate could be to remove knowledge mediators of interculturality – teachers and researchers who force feed students with their ideological fantasies. Intercultural education *without force feeders!*
    [It is important to dream at times… Education without educators and 'educatees'? Education beyond education?]

六十二

These voices that openly express self-critique in decolonial endeavours are commendable. Decolonial readings may often ignore one's efforts for redressing power asymmetries while holding others accountable. One of the instances of decolonial self-examination, that I see to be inspiring, is Moosavi's (2023, p. 137) critique of his own attempts to decolonize the curriculum and how they were actually limited since "the course may have inadvertently: (a) sustained exclusion while claiming to be inclusive; (b) maintained the status quo while claiming to be radical, and (c) reinscribed Westerncentrism while claiming to decolonize".

六十三

We may argue that some Southern scholars feel the need to be associated with universities in the Anglo-sphere as evidence of the veracity of their epistemic labour; yet, another important factor is that scholars are simply looking for better rights, conditions and benefits. Academic mobility may help scholars to develop more profound epistemic stances by drawing intersections as they navigate the various epistemologies from both South and North (Kim, 2014).

六十四

Saturnalia needed in intercultural research whereby servants become masters! During this festival in Ancient Rome, enslaved people were allowed to sit at the head of the table and were served by their masters. We could all learn from Saturnalia of interculturality.

六十五

Decolonial attitude is not linear and straightforward but more of anticolonial political commitments that refute the possibility of interculturality by simply encouraging teachers and students to centre discourses around knowledge, skills, identity, self, other, etc.

六十六

I am not a big fan of these 'innocence' claims. Simply because one is subaltern, it does not make it acceptable to function beyond 'ethics' and 'morals'.

六十七

The most difficult thing to do when one works on interculturality in education and research is to refrain oneself from giving orders.

六十八

Our logics are subjectively logical. We do not share the same logics and we are indeed creators of our logics that are not readily available out there. We navigate and create whatever seems to entertain our politics.

六十九

Ideological is always *the other*. We are all ideologically inclined, even in our refusal to be…

七十

Research on interculturality should shake and shock us – not comfort us in our own 'safe space'!

七十一

Economic violence speaks to me more than *social injustice*. Today's injustice is systematically embedded in the economic.

七十二

Interculturality is the theory of humans creating, perpetuating and exercising systems of privilege/subordination.

七十三

Some papers express some thought-provoking ideas in the sense that one is shaken, thrown and shocked. Dunlap (2022: 1) claims that anarchist decolonial perspectives need to be encouraged since "they articulate permanent tensions against divisions of labour, hierarchies, statist-colonial organizational forms, and industrial/digital technologies"; reading through without preconceived disinclination from radically-sound approaches is certainly recommended. Very strong and well-made insights.

[Anarchism as a much-needed 'swearword'.]

七十四

A China supporter from Mainland explains to an aggressive American journalist: "Chinese people don't want war – they want to make money, they want to own an apartment, they want to have a nice and happy life… no war!". The honesty is refreshing! I wish we interculturalists were so direct! *Money, money, money.*

七十五

Skewed geopolitics of knowledge are not exclusive to any field, but they are more of a characteristic feature of a wide array of academic disciplines, e.g., philosophy, global health, communication studies and education.

七十六

Always a feeling of schizophrenia listening to 'our' critiques in intercultural communication education. We call for decentring, the postcolonial, the posthuman and yet the voices we use are still very US-centric and 'white'.

七十七

We need to find the freedom to explain and understand how we 'do' interculturality.

七十八

The pleasure of writing a book about interculturality. It is like walking and running in a forest – all this fresh air, all these animals, these insects, these plants, these flowers and these colours. They invigorate and soothe you. It is just you and them, and the traces of others who have passed before you.

Writing a journal article about interculturality is like exercising at the gym. It's noisy routine. It's a straight line. Uncreative. A factory full of neoliberal and dull bodies. The strongest show off their muscles, organs and bodies in the changing room. But in the end, they all want to look the same – same muscles, same organs, same bodies.

七十九

Merely congratulating each other on new publications on interculturality without discussing and debating the content in depth is counter-productive. A new publication in itself is always the beginning… Next time do not congratulate anyone without finding faults with their work… this is the only way forward! We cannot be self-complacent with interculturality.

八十

Every thought, every notion, every ideology, every book/article is inestimable for reflecting on interculturality. Confront everything with everything by letting them enter and trouble your and their worlds!

八十一

Interculturality is far away from hard sciences and its scientificity would not be affirmed by eschewing philosophical paradigms in navigating its complexities.

八十二

Interpretation should not be fixed in particular cultural constructions of creative practices since there is also a space for self-construction.

八十三

Art, like interculturality, is ideological too. I see an exhibition of a Pakistan-born American artist in China. I do not particularly like the art pieces I see. Reading through their descriptions in Chinese and English, I get frustrated. They are full of Americanisms, American ideological discourses on identity politics. I can feel the words. A Chinese friend who is visiting the exhibition with me does not see this. I am somewhat surprised by the chasms between the paintings (somewhat 'different' looking aesthetically and visually compared to 'Western' art I have seen – whatever 'Western' art might mean). The art has its originality. However, the accompanying discourses are mere copy-pasting of current identity ideological positionings dominant in the US and some parts of the Western world. Art is ideological too. Art is discourse. But it can diverge from words sometimes.

[Often interculturality faces the same problem. People's experiences of it might differ entirely from the way they 'discourse' around it by copy-pasting bits and pieces of (often dominating) ideological orders to do so.]

八十四

Maybe intercultural research should be about exploring and combining what we consider as unreconcilable – just like the realities of interculturality.

八十五

'Otherwise' as a slogan in relation to how we (asked to) 'do' interculturality.

八十六

Literature is the type of text that does not spend a lot of time and words to move something in you. As much as academia is rigorous, a lot of people would always feel that literature represents the human experience. The experience of overwhelming misery or happiness; the experience of feeling absolutely nothing; the experience of not knowing what one feels.

八十七

Is the solution to the riddle of interculturality not to do anything about interculturality? Stop (half-clumsily) defining it, stop (half-clumsily) positioning yourself towards it, stop ordering about it. Interculturality as the non-action *par excellence*. Let it happen.

八十八

Fragments are the perfect examples of how human minds work. Fragments are people and their ephemeral ideas, feelings and outlooks. Writing streamlined texts train the brains to work in certain ways. Do fragments remind us of our humanity, disorganization and unmethodicality? do fragments represent methodical unmethodicality?

八十九

I see a necklace containing a piece of defected porcelain. My first reaction is awe. It looks very beautiful, the 'faulty' piece giving it a very special 'flavour'.

I am tempted to say the 'broken' piece gives the untouched piece of porcelain its charm. But isn't it the other way around? *Think* otherwise?

九十

Let's lose ourselves. No need to look for anything. *Wander!*

[Shouldering thoughts backstage]

This last section introduces fragments that have to do with more personal elements and calls for the researcher's autobiography to find its way into their own research (and teaching!). The fragments present some of our interrogations, doubts, wishes, dreams and insecurities.

○

Books on interculturality do contain aspects of our autobiography, often hiding behind our ideas, word uses, references (to 'gurus'), hesitations, critiques, contradictions, etc. The act of having written a book on interculturality also constitutes part of our own autobiographies.

[A book that does not include the author's own engagement with interculturality while writing, researching interculturality, is ignoring, pretending to 'do' and 'care about' interculturality.]

一

Literature is fresh air. Academia would hardly ever level up to the epistemological nuance and depth of literature.

二

There is a lot I want to say, but I am the first one to exercise censorship. I cannot risk it all because I am vulnerable and I do not afford to.

[(Self-)censorship is not rare in intercultural communication education and research. I remember being told once during a very 'painful' keynote speech in Italy where I had been critically evaluating dominating 'models' of intercultural competence that "I should not do this kind of work; such models are central for 'democracy', 'human rights'..." – with the utterer turning his back to me for the rest of the keynote in protest... Young people sitting at the back of the room dared to speak against this 'local' guru who appeared to be more of a politician than a 'scholar' (but *can a scholar act beyond politics?*).]

三

When I am more senior with more social and economic capitals, I will probably make bolder but logically sound and scientifically substantiated statements.

[I wonder if 'logically' is a Western construct? Whose logic are we refer-ring to when we use the word?]

四

Some individuals may take pleasure in downplaying their own race, culture and language but I do not. I rather openly discuss aspects to be improved but would always emphasize how the subaltern should not be blamed for their misgivings. It is not a matter of colour, knowledges and/or skills but a ques-tion of who has what and what things they are willing to do to maintain that state of affairs.

[I often hear myself essentializing 'my' people ('white people') in my cri-tiques of intercultural scholarship… not being too sure of who it is that I am referring to.]

五.

I am Moroccan and I cannot venture to claim that I know my people since some individuals act totally outside the cultural box and normativities cele-brated in our society. In fact, Moroccans are increasingly reflecting modernity and westernization according to the pillars of Europe and the US. It is nearly impossible to unsettle the waves of westernization and modernity as defined by the Anglo-sphere.

六

I have always tried to write literature myself even before I joined academia. I read Mohammed Choukri and Dostoevsky at first which set the bar very high. I do not enjoy the literature on the sky, flowers, colours and imaginative beauty. I enjoy texts that address what aches in me.

七

Writing critical scholarships, or at least what we think is critical, raises an un-deniable sense of insecurity about one's rhetorics and actions. I am always ex-ercising self-doubt around my legitimacy in saying what I say and whether my doings are in congruence with my literature. Since the majority of my works are decolonial and/or postcolonial (R'boul, 2021, 2022a,b,c), this is even more convoluted and sensitive. Although this insecurity can be painful, I think all scholars need to experience such scepticism about their works. It does not help to broadcast rigidity, self-centredness and total certainty of our ways of knowing and insights. We all need to act human and continuously revamp and question our perspectives and opinions. It does not impinge on one's reputation and/or epistemic capacity to question one's stances and insights.

[Insecurities about one's work could be discussed with others in so-called safe spaces. I often share my insecurities about what I say and write with my PhD students and a couple of colleagues – and in some of my writing. Feelings of being an impostor also serve to remind us of how 'small' we are in front of interculturality.]

八

I have learned a lot in Morocco; I have learned that expecting others to do you favours is not the right way of navigating. I have learned that I need to make extra efforts to assert my epistemic capacity since 'race' has codified differences in the sense that some people are designated to have a natural gift to be superior.

九

The anger at seeing past co-authors abuse my name by 'erasing' and/or 'dissimulating' it to make believe that they have a long list of publications and achievements, and to get a promotion – and thus more money. I used to be very generous in the past, in the name of interculturality and especially future 'intercultural dialogue'. Some of them wrote very little in these publications and yet their names are there for everyone to see. *Reminder: do more research on fabricating intercultural trust.*

十

The very realization that my works are getting more recognition while looking back at where I come from is overwhelming. The setbacks are as important as our achievements. Resistance, thick skin and resilience are crucial in academia.

十一

I can safely say that my parents are not the most intercultural beings. They sometimes share some assumptions that are clearly biased and might be racist. They take them for granted as a lot of people share the same perspectives. It is an interesting conversation trying to draw my parents' attention to debates going on for a while in interculturality. As Moroccan Arabic (Darija) does not supply equivalents for a number of essential notions in interculturality given my western socialization into academia and literature, I do struggle to communicate my ideas. This realization made me reconsider the extent to which our scholarships are accessible to non-specialist people. Interculturality is supposed to intervene but it is quite problematic to make a difference when our own rhetorics are esoteric. However, interculturality should not explain because its premises are entirely about rectifying and rebalancing human relations.

十二

Those who soar are often belittled by those who cannot fly.

十三

On several occasions in 2022, I heard some 'Western' country leaders refer to Russia and China as *adversaries* and *competitors*. The mask has dropped… The business aspects of current conflicts seem far too transparent… Can there be 'peace' without money involved?

十四

Virus politics continues three years on after 2020. Some countries decide to not allow people from certain countries not to enter their borders. Passport-based only. But anyone from these countries is free to cross. *Bio-politicization of self-other, of interculturality.*

十五

If I spend a substantial amount of time mourning and complaining, readers may get frustrated and upset because I remind them of what they do not want to experience or see. Struggles are always there, and the very fact that we may turn a blind eye to them or avoid seeing them does not undo them. [The 'happification' of research and education might be leading us to a catastrophe.]

十六

Relocating to Hong Kong feels like the most 'intercultural' experience possible. The city has its own vibrancy, attitude and dynamic of interculturality. Coming from Morocco, it feels like coming into a whole new universe. Again, this could be due to my lack of international travel but these insights could be pertinent to other individuals in the Global South.

十七

My hope for Hong Kong is that the systems of privilege and subordination will be alleviated.

十八

Shrines are an interesting place in Morocco; they are spheres where the unusual is unleashed. I am hoping to invite Fred to witness some traditions that have historical groundings in the culture and have some occult logics. It would be exciting to navigate with Fred how these practices could tell us about interculturality, especially noting how the rationales behind these rituals could be hardly explained and conveyed to the others. I am hoping to explore how the potential sense of exoticism is a principal factor behind a lot of intercultural encounters.

Conclusions

This chapter has unveiled 'further intuitions' to continue exploring and problematizing interculturality. We have thought in e.g. metaphors and neologisms, sharing our own uncertainties, (further) hesitations, critiques and openings to do so. As researchers and educators, we cannot continue to pretend that the interculturality that we observe, analyse, teach about and 'dictate' constitutes a 'separate' bubble of encounters over which we have complete control. As researchers and educators, we are part of the equilibrium that e.g. research participants create and unfold in front of our eyes and ears. Ethically speaking, this requires from us recognizing and taking into account our own influences, preferences, silencing and biases in dealing with interculturality. The chapter has also insisted on the crucial issue of languaging, i.e. caring about the ways we speak and engage around the notion linguistically, in one or several languages, listening very attentively to what others and ourselves have to say about interculturality. No one can ever be ready to 'do', understand and examine such simplex phenomena filled with potential contradictions, manipulations and instabilities.

[Think further]

Write down five anaphoric fragments destabilizing your takes on what interculturality might mean/be.

Explain to yourself and others the following fragment: 'Interculturality is a constantly co-constructed changing self-other-portrait'.

During your next interactions with different kinds of people, observe how 'verbal seesaw' is occurring. What strategies do you seem to be using to balance/unbalance what you do and say with others? How about them?

Would you agree that we have a tendency in research and education to try to control and 'outwit' interculturality? Can you think of concrete examples (and counter-examples!) from the literature and e.g., your own teaching?

In the section [Adopting Lateral Thinking], one fragment is urging us to experience 'radical imagination' about the world of intercultural research and education being dominated by 'Africa'. Reflect on your *intuitions* after reading this fragment: what differences would such reversal of epistemic, economic and ideological power relations make for you in relation to intercultural scholarship and education?

[Main keywords]

Equilibrium: Balance and imbalance are constitutive of any intercultural encounter. Through what we say and do, we push and pull each other endlessly in all kinds of directions. Although we may have the impression that someone might have 'won' or 'done' interculturality in a *successful* way, this is only temporary and probably erroneous. As soon as we move to another context, discursive and ideological sphere, interlocutor, language, etc. we become axisymmetric (shapes and sizes are never exactly the same). The Latin word *equilibrium* contains *libra* for *a balance, a pair of scales*. It is not meant to symbolize a horizontal position here but a constantly renegotiated place of negotiations. Equilibrium applies to the very acts of researching and educating for interculturality too.

Homophones: From Greek for *same + sound*. A homophone refers to two words pronounced alike and yet different in e.g. spelling and meaning (e.g. flour vs flower). Since English appears to be the global language of 'academic' interculturality, there is a tendency for us to speak as if words meant the same when translated into the language from our different languages. And yet, we are constantly faced with homophones in intercultural research and education: words that might look the same and yet mean completely different things. In order to ensure communicating around interculturality in more or less satisfactory ways (without believing that one can communicate 'perfectly'), let's pause on every word that we use in English, treating them like potential homophones.

***Interculturalese*:** This is a synonym for the idea of *interculturalspeak* (Dervin, 2016) which describes automatic, un-reflexive and 'empty-while-loaded' discursive engagements with interculturality in research and education. The repetition of keywords, popular 'concepts' and 'ideas', namedropping, leads to *interculturalese. A flow of words which makes interculturality a clearly ideologically oriented notion that does not recognize itself as such.*

Language in the making: Producing knowledge about interculturality must be considered as something that is bound to change and move in all directions.

Linguistically, it means accepting to try out different ways of discoursing, speaking about interculturality, trying out *language in the making*. As much as interculturality is an unstable construct, languaging it should reflect its instabilities and the changes it forces us to experience.

Libido dominandi: From Latin: *Lust for domination*, the will to power. Considering today's neoliberal scholarship, pushing everyone to achieve some kind of (global and local) influence in research, teaching and society, disseminating whatever we might think we can contribute, being 'out there' on social media, creating 'models', recycling and rehearsing 'concepts', being part of specific (glocal) 'tribes', urge us in-/directly to develop some form of 'will to power'. Citations, invitations to speak, committee memberships, editorships, etc. all contribute (willy-nilly) to this phenomenon.

(The) limitless: *Interculturality has no end.* No one can ever be ready for it or 'doing' it, speaking about it in 'proper' ways [Proper cannot but be ideological here]. Interculturality pushes us to not rest, take things for granted, claim victory.

(The) origami of languages: From Japanese for *folding paper*, origami is often described as the art of paper-folding, shaping a sheet of paper into an object or an animal without e.g. gluing or taping. Considering the complexities of communicating around interculturality in English and other languages, we must examine the folds of each word that we have constructed individually and/or with others, without using glue or tape that would 'seal' the meanings and connotations of these words.

Slogan words: The word *slogan* is from Gaelic for Battle Cry (etymonline. org, 2023). A short and catchy phrase, a slogan is meant to create an appeal and to attract the attention of people. As an economic-political notion that is used to determine 'our' being and becoming together, interculturality often falls on the verge of the *sloganesque*. Concepts, ideas, names, 'theories' and 'models' often serve the purpose of slogans in intercultural education and research (e.g. "you cannot use the concept of race in research on interculturality, even when you work on racism").

Trompe l'oeil: From French for 'deceiving the eyes'. If not careful enough, we might be blinded and pushed to misinterpret, misunderstand and misuse certain ideological positions, hidden in language, when dealing with interculturally glocally. For instance, the ideologies of 'democratic culture' or 'culture confidence' can easily turn into *trompe l'oeil* by their appeal which requires examining them carefully.

Verbal seesaw: A seesaw is a long, flat board resting on a platform in the middle. Two individuals balance the board by going up and down in turns. A verbal seesaw in intercultural research and education reminds us of the importance to re-negotiate constantly the ways we engage with interculturality together *in words*, not being satisfied with the ways things are formulated in e.g. English as a global language, pushing ourselves to be as transparent as possible about the connotations of the words that we use.

References

Abdul-Jabbar, W. Kh (2022). *Medieval Muslim Philosophers and Intercultural Communication: Towards a Dialogical Paradigm in Education*. London: Routledge.

Bateye, B., Masaeli, M., Muller, L., & Roothaan, A. (eds.) (2023). *Beauty in African Thought: Critical Perspectives on the Western Idea of Development*. Lanham, MD, Boulder, CO, New York, London: Lexington Books.

Dervin, F. (2016). *Interculturality in Education: A Theoretical and Methodological Toolbox*. London: Palgrave.

Dervin, F. (2021). *Critical and Reflexive Languaging in the Construction of Interculturality as an Object of Research and Practice* (19 April 2021). Digital series of talks on plurilingualism and interculturality, University of Copenhagen.

Dervin, F. (2022) *Interculturality in Fragments: A Reflexive Approach*. Singapore: Springer.

Dervin, F., & Jacobsson, A. (2022). *Intercultural Communication Education. Broken Realities and Rebellious Dreams*. London: Springer.

Dervin, F., & Yuan, M. (2021). *Revitalizing Interculturality in Education: Chinese Minzu as a Companion*. London: Routledge.

Descola, Ph. (2013). *Beyond Nature and Culture*. Chicago, IL: Chicago University Press.

Dunlap, A. (2022). 'I don't want your progress! It tries to kill … me!' Decolonial encounters and the anarchist critique of civilization. *Globalizations*. DOI: 10.1080/14747731.2022.2073657.

etymonline.org (2023). Slogan.

Hocking, D. (2018). *Communicating Creativity: The Discursive Facilitation of Creative Activity in Arts*. Basingstoke: Palgrave Macmillan. DOI: 10.1057/978-1-137-55804-6

Hondzel, C. D., & Gulliksen, M. S. (2015). Culture and creativity: Examining variations in divergent thinking within Norwegian and Canadian communities. *SAGE Open*. DOI: 10.1177/2158244015611448.

House, J., Kadar, D. Z., Liu, F., & Han, D. (2022). The problem of translating Chinese policy-related expressions: A case study of *wenming* ('civilised'). *Text & Talk*. OnlineFirst.

Hsu, H.-Y. (2022). How do Chinese people evaluate "Tang-Ping" (lying flat) and effort-making: The moderation effect of return expectation. *Frontiers in Psychology*, 13, 871439. DOI: 10.3389/fpsyg.2022.871439.

Kim, T. (2014). The intellect, mobility and epistemic positioning in doing comparisons and comparative education. *Comparative Education*, 50(1), 58–72. DOI: 10.1080/03050068.2013.874237.

Kristeva, J. (2004). *Thinking about Liberty in Dark Times*. Bergen: The Holberg Prize Seminar 2004, University of Bergen.

Liu, F., Han, D., House, J., & Kadar, D. Z. (2021). The expressions '(M)minzu-zhuyi' and 'Nationalism': A contrastive pragmatic analysis. *Journal of Pragmatics* 174, 168–178.

Maldonado-Torres, N. (2007). On the coloniality of being. *Cultural Studies*, 21(2–3), 240–270. DOI: 10.1080/09502380601162548.

Marín-Arrese, J. I. (2011). Epistemic legitimizing strategies, commitment and accountability in discourse. *Discourse Studies*, 13(6), 789–797. DOI: 10.1177/1461445611421360c.

McCarthy, C., & Dimitriadis, G. (2000). The work of art in the postcolonial imagination. *Discourse: Studies in the Cultural Politics of Education*, 21(1), 59–74. DOI: 10.1080/01596300050005501.

Mignolo, W. (2018). Foreward. On pluriversality and multipolarity. In B. Reiter (Ed.), *Constructing the Pluriverse: The Geopolitics of Knowledge* (pp. ix–xvi). Durham, NC and London: Duke University Press.

Moosavi, L. (2023). Turning the decolonial gaze towards ourselves: Decolonising the curriculum and 'decolonial reflexivity' in sociology and social theory. *Sociology*, 57(1), 137–156. DOI: 10.1177/00380385221096037.

Mourgues, C., Barbot, B., Tan, M., & Grigorenko, E. L. (2015). The interaction between culture and the development of creativity. In L. A. Jensen (Ed.), *The Oxford Handbook of Human Development and Culture: An Interdisciplinary Perspective* (pp. 255–270). Oxford: Oxford University Press. DOI: 10.1093/oxfordhb/9780199948550.013.16.

Olofsson, J. K., & Wilson, D. A. (2018). Human olfaction: It takes two villages. *Current Biology*, 28(3), R108–R110.

Oramo, S. (2020). Composer focus. https://www.barbican.org.uk/read-watch-listen/composer-focus-sakari-oramo-on-jean-sibelius

Quijano, A. (2000). Coloniality of power and eurocentrism in Latin America. *International Sociology*, 15(2), 215–232. DOI: 10.1177/0268580900015002005.

Quijano, A. (2007). Coloniality and modernity/rationality. *Cultural Studies*, 21(2–3), 168–178. DOI: 10.1080/09502380601164353.

R'boul, H. (2021). North/south imbalances in intercultural communication education. *Language and Intercultural Communication*, 21(2), 144–157. DOI: 10.1080/14708477.2020.1866593.

R'boul, H. (2022a). Postcolonial interventions in intercultural communication knowledge: Meta-intercultural ontologies, decolonial knowledges and epistemological polylogue. *Journal of International and Intercultural Communication*, 15(1), 75–93. DOI: 10.1080/17513057.2020.1829676.

R'boul, H. (2022b). Intercultural philosophy and internationalisation of higher education: Epistemologies of the South, geopolitics of knowledge and epistemological polylogue. *Journal of Further and Higher Education*, 46(8), 1149–1160. DOI: 10.1080/0309877X.2022.2055451.

R'boul, H. (2022c). Epistemological plurality in intercultural communication knowledge. *Journal of Multicultural Discourses*, 17(2), 173–188. DOI: 10.1080/17447143.2022.2069784.

R'boul, H. (2023). Intercultivism and alternative knowledges in intercultural education. *Globalisation, Societies and Education*. DOI: 10.1080/14767724.2023.2166018

R'boul, H., Dervin, F., & Saidi, B. (2023). South-South acculturation: Majority-group students' relation to Sub-Saharan students in Moroccan universities. *International Journal of Intercultural Relations*, 96. https://doi.org/10.1016/j.ijintrel.2023.101834

Roucek, J. S. (1944). A history of the concept of ideology. *Journal of the History of Ideas*, 5(4), 479–488.

Said, E. (1972). *Orientalism*. London: Penguin Classics.

Shao, Y., et al. (2019). How does culture shape creativity? A mini-review. *Frontiers in Psychology*, 10, 1–8. DOI: 10.3389/fpsyg.2019.01219.

Sidnell, J. (2012). Who knows best? Evidentiality and epistemic asymmetry in conversation. *Pragmatics and Society*, 3(2), 294–320. DOI: 10.1075/ps.3.2.08sid.

Tian, X., & Dervin, F. (2023). Intercultural communication education beyond 'Western' democracy-talk? Zhongyong as a way of decentring democracy-based teaching. In J. Zajda, P. Hallam, & J. Whitehouse (Eds.), *Globalisation, Values Education and Teaching Democracy* (pp. 143–157). Singapore: Springer International Publishing AG.

Xiaojun, Z. (2017). The paradigmatic crises in China's Minzu studies: Reflections from the perspective of human development. *Journal of Chinese Humanities*, 3, 135–155.

5 Conclusion

Interculturality is not a metaphor

Our unfinished business to look elsewhere

This book marks our *unfinished business* in creating novel lenses and perspectives that allow the readers to expand their horizons with us about interculturality research and education. It is our third joint project and it continues the traditions of analysis employed in the previous two books (Dervin & R'boul, 2022; R'boul & Dervin, 2023). We are committed to pursuing more profound lines of inquiry that take interculturality research and education from a field that is limited to surface analysis preoccupied with competence, awareness and understanding to an epistemic terrain in which interculturality is incessantly unpacked, disrupted and rethought through sociology, philosophy and knowledge studies (amongst others). Boilerplate knowledges, texts and codes are not the answers despite their cosy pleasure. The normative expectations around intercultural scholars are to rehearse certain ideologies and notions to situate oneself within a cabal. Looking elsewhere would never be a finished process since its rationales are adamant. While fragments throughout the book could entail vehement critiques, they are not loud cries and/or sentiments of exasperation but calls for the field to cut ties with some deeply rooted tendencies to sound and speak alike. Fragments are a series of electrical cardioversion with high-energy critique and deconstruction to reset a normal and healthy rhythm for moving forward. We may be collectively moving forward but in different ways; what matters is how genuine these ways are – as well as our intentions.

We rarely construct complete truths by instant illumination but only through fragment by fragment, partial glimpses, on a continuous, random and small scale by successive developments like a laborious mosaic (Nin, 2017). This book has its own personality that is often not controlled or conditioned by ourselves since fragments are tracing the passages of mind with a series of infinite discords. Fragments and interculturality are the sides of the same coins overlapping their complexities and carrying their conjunctions within the text and beyond. That is, fragments reinforce the (im)possibility of capturing interculturality in symmetrical sequences, logical build-up and

DOI: 10.4324/9781003458050-5

harmonious rational melodies through visual dissections and ricochets. This book manages to combine the visual, the textual and the epistemic in representing the inherent intricacies of interculturality as a phenomenon relating to the self's alterity through other selves (a reference to a temporary definition of interculturality by one of us). A second layer of complexity is that we speak for and within one voice without boundaries or intentions to make outlines for who is speaking what; readers are encouraged not to pursue dividing lines in their readings but rather rejoice at the (co)(di)vergences as reflections of *interculturality in exercising interculturality* while enunciating about interculturality. The book embraces intuitions, hesitations and doubts as normal and expected developments in making sense of interculturality.

We see the truth only in fragments (Beecher, 1869) and interculturality pushes us to see the truth in our fragmented selves, especially when the other self tends to work through our devices. Writing in unconventional forms can force one to think in unusual modalities and formats making use of questioning, self-critique and irony to realize alternative knowledges. It is challenging to look elsewhere when our enunciations are mired in the mainstream although we exhibit an exceptional readiness to move beyond what is dominant. The first time Fred mentioned that he wrote a book exclusively composed of fragments, Hamza questioned how this form of output could replace linear and organized academic texts. It was only when Hamza read Fred's book *Interculturality in Fragments* (2022) that he realized how fragments provided the core elements for discussion, supported by additional details that expand the fragments' epistemological substance. Then, the idea of the book emerged, and Hamza started to jot down fragments every day to feel a sense of emancipation from the rigid standards, rules and conventions of what academic texts are supposed to look and sound like. Hamza appreciates Fred's invitation to join him in further unravelling interculturality as a theory of everything. The process of writing the book was as 'different', 'unusual' and 'irregular' for Hamza as some of the readers may feel while reading the book. Similarly, for Fred, (re-)reading through and being confronted with another scholar's fragments about interculturality was represented both as confusing and enriching experience since he had only seen his own previous publications containing fragments in the field of interculturality. Following months of exciting discussions and negotiations around the fragments, he believes that this genre is worth exploring further by scholars, educators and students.

We would like to remind the readers that "what sticks to memory, often, are those odd little fragments that have no beginning and no end" (O'Brien, 2009: 34). While we may peruse entire books, there are sections, paragraphs and fragments that define these texts as a whole. One fragment may shape our perspective and opinion of a piece of writing. One fragment and one shot may disrupt the readers to reconsider everything they have come to know. We believe that there is still a lot of work ahead and we feel that our 'responsibility' of drawing people's attention to what matters about interculturality has not been fulfilled yet – will it ever be? We think that as soon as the book is published, it transcends the authors and becomes at the mercy of the readers as the fragments are always open to interpretation and they are not bound by time and space. As soon as the book is out, it belongs to the readers who can leave their marks *on* (annotations) and *around* it (citations, critiques, potential plagiat…). The academic market requires us to leave our trace on the book by adding our names to the cover. However, like artists who do not sign their names on a canvas, leaving no trace of their 'ownership', we dream of an academic where a book could be 'nameless' – a book for all to own fully. As much as interculturality does not belong to 'Hamza' or 'Fred', it does not belong to 'you', 'them' or 'us' (see Barthes, 2020 on the 'death of the author'). Ideas contained in a fragmentary book like this one that navigate and fluctuate. A fragmentary book like this one asks us to give up our static and frozen sense of ownership and identity. *Things can only be temporary.* If they are not, they are not about 'research' – from Latin *re* (*again, back*) and *circare* (*go about, wander, traverse*, see the word *circus*).

While there are some cues that may specify the tone and gist of the fragment, we opted to leave some space for readers to complete the book at least in their minds and imaginations. Interculturality is still a work in process and cannot be reduced to deterministic chunks of knowledge that seek comfort. We do not recommend picking up these fragments and 'glueing' them together to have a mended whole as they are standalone knowledges and their 'uniqueness' resides in their isolation. We encourage readers to disagree with us and not perceive our fragments as ends in themselves but rather versions of our social realities. We invite readers to consider our future works which will build on what has been done so far.

Interculturality does not have a synonym

Interculturality is not a metaphor to denote any approximation of a limited set of experiences of communicating, engaging and interacting with the other. Interculturality cannot be processed through benevolent and benign synonyms that *wipe the sky with a glove* – a Moroccan popular saying that emphasizes how some people tend to reduce complex phenomena to simplistic interpretations and solutions. Interculturality is not a swappable term for ensuring the smooth functioning of intercultural relations, but rather a notion that covers whatever is in-between and reflects back on the self and the other. Fred and Hamza continuously discuss and critique some perspectives and practices that they perceive to be indoctrinating (the authors' next project) because they are quite distant from what interculturality is genuinely about – although indoctrination is also a common component of the notion. Subscribing to a version of interculturality that is politically neutral and/or epistemologically imposing deviates attention from the core issues and the profound analyses of self-alterity through other selves. We imagine that the notion itself could be emptied from its essence when it is repetitively and randomly used to imply other things that are superficially *intercultural*. By using interculturality as a metaphor in our stances and practices, we are indeed refusing to offer an opportunity for others to move beyond us to maintain our discourses could be the most *non-intercultural* act.

Hamza and Fred may not necessarily share the same perspective of interculturality but their convergences include the pursuit of interventions that cripple inequalities and injustices either in conversation or reality. Most of the fragments in the book are about justice, but not particular manifestations of justice that are convenient and peaceful. For a lot of systems and individuals, justice could be a violent word suggesting stripping them of their power. Justice could be a risky business when its fundamental premises are to shift away from the unilateral interpretation of social realities and the type of measures to be implemented to redress asymmetries. Interculturality is not a metaphor to discuss only what is convenient. These critiques broach some questions around the ethos of interculturality: *it is a field of analysing or intervening?* Readers could have a say in this; we would welcome reactions from readers to specific fragments and the questions we ask. Interculturality does not have a synonym unless we decide to clutch the theorizations that have been demolished, that we rather ignore the available literature only to engage in self-feeding endeavours to twist arguments and turn a blind eye to the remarkable developments, especially in Fred's numerous books. While interculturality is no one's property, we should not deliberately overlook what challenges us and unsettles our assumptions running the risk of putting the field of interculturality on hold.

Hamza recalls his trips on the MTR (The Mass Transit Railway) in Hong Kong from home to his university and the constant re-appraisal of his ideas and theories as he is looking around at the others and their looks back. Hamza came to realize that we are often tossed within interculturality with minimum control of its undertakings. Also, Fred reflects on his frequent sits at a park in China and his experiences with local people and how they shake his conceptions of human communication through space and time. All these 'moments' are represented in the book in that the authors share their personal stories (which is not very common in academia) to remind the readers that they are people as well, who oscillate between hesitations and doubts. The authors are probably not very confident, as may be imagined in some readers' minds, in their intercultural 'skills' despite their literature. They could be the individuals who lack 'confidence' in their abilities (the most) to navigate intercultural encounters since they are piercingly conscious of the complexities inherent in interculturality. Again: *what do we want out of interculturality?* The answer is 'it depends'. It depends on our visions, aspirations and objectives. Do we want to place ourselves over others to teach them how to interculturalize? Or do we want to keep digging into the endless process of intellectual productions so as to understand *a bit better* – without ever claiming that we really know *what interculturality is about and what it entails*?

Interculturality should not be a metaphor that depends on deficiency discourses portraying teachers, students, individuals and communities as e.g. lacking appropriate non-essentialist knowledge. These people are not in need of some interculturality narratives with false ('western') promises of e.g. *progress, democracy* and *equality*. Interculturality is about co-constructing knowledge together in order to compile the pieces (again and again) for broader interventions. Hamza argues that it is quite easy to conduct an 'assessment' of Moroccan students' intercultural competence to highlight deficiencies and ultimately build on these explanations to call out teachers for a lack of intercultural awareness. Why do we keep pretending that there is one version of interculturality that is accessible, tangible and assessable? Why do we make use of dominating voices from 'global' academia (which might be far from 'global') to impose *one* such version? Hamza keeps receiving invitations from some Moroccan PhD students to work on intercultural competence just to reply that it is a zombie concept that 'interculturality' has already wrecked. These students tend to be surprised that a scholar specialized in interculturality does not believe in the *doctrine* of intercultural competence. Fred has also faced similar reactions when he has suggested moving away from the 'taken-for-granted', the 'obvious' and the 'guruesque', which only tends to apply mechanically the *re-* (as in repetition) of *research*.

[*Re-search*: go about, wander *ad infinitum*.]

We hope that readers will take it upon themselves to look elsewhere for the sake of moving forward. Some of these questions could be of help:

- What is my own definition of interculturality at moment X and moment Y and with others?
- Is interculturality metaphysics, a phenomenon, an analytical lens or an end in itself (or all these at the same time)?
- What are my perspectives beyond the 'big' names' theories and stances? How do I relate my personal experiences, pains, impressions, relations and scientific takes on the notion?
- What is interculturality for me taking into account my conditions, standing and place?
- What critical readings have I developed over the course of reading this book on the various *interculturalities* available?
- What alternative modalities of thinking and writing can I draw on to construct novel insights? How could I make sure that my re-construction does not fully satisfy my thinking and stop?
- How do I imagine the future of the interculturality field moving forward?
- How can we undermine the use of interculturality as a metaphor with substantial ideological loadings?

Interculturality does not have an antonym

Systematic rationalities within interculturality may fall short in capturing its nuances; interculturality is playful, which warrants some artistic and creative lenses that centre playfulness in the sense that all dimensions are continuously revamped, denied, emphasized and reshaped. As much as interculturality does not have a synonym, it does not have any antonym either since the lack/absence of interculturality could constitute the *most intercultural* act. That is, interculturality is inclusive of those racist, supremacist and negative attitudes towards oneself and others. We are always the other of the other; we are constantly working through precise analogies that assign some credibility to whatever is conceivable and fathomable. All works on interculturality need to be labelled as "work in progress" even when the most impeccable reasoning and argumentation are diffused. We are bound by rationality but interculturality is ultimately *irrational* (Dervin, 2022). Why should interculturality be particular when one of the most brilliant scholars can only offer a 'temporary' definition when others speak with authority? Interculturality is being abused and often used in ways that could be described as *antonyms*. Interculturality does not have an antonym but using interculturality to dominate is indeed an antonym. Hamza feels that some of his insights are absurd because they may supply the understanding that "here I am, I know what interculturality is about". As such Hamza remembers his parents' piece of advice to always speak well of Morocco in front of others. His parents are way wiser than he thought. They just claimed a remarkable insight: "do not try to look good in the eyes of others by disdaining your people; you will neither look good in their eyes nor in those of your people".

Hamza's parents probably see merit in Choukri's quote in his renowned novel *For Bread Alone*: "Oran is exile and Tetuan is imprisonment. And since I am happier in Tetuan than in Oran, that means I prefer jail in my native land to freedom in exile" (Choukri, 2007: 68). This quote is illustrative of how some people tend to interculturalize; the tendency to stick to oneself regardless of the other' perks; this would need more unpacking but for the time being, *freedom is always a priority*. Is interculturality freedom? Do/can we choose to interculturalize? Do/can we choose how our interculturalities take place? Is essentialism in interculturality freedom: freedom to situate all people in one basket? Interculturality may be freedom for some but imprisonment for others especially when you are at the receiving end of inequalities. Every intercultural encounter is unequal and imbalanced; that is why the question is who defines the terms, conditions and rules? Going back to the idea of antonym, it is often funny when someone tells us "do not care about the other, just ignore" while our entire works are about the other and their relation to us. Would interculturality still be meaningful when the other is denied? Probably yes, because that is real-life interculturality rather than embellished discourses around competence, citizenship and democracy. We need to be aware that some people cannot afford to resonate with some perspectives because they are detached from their realities. As much as interculturality could be *tourism, fun* and *playfulness* with the other, it could also entail pain, doubts and hesitations for others.

Interculturality could be the theory of navigating the outside world (see Dervin, 2023). Sitting on a bench in Beijing without communicating with anybody is indeed interculturality. Silence is only superficial, making sense and negotiating is always taking place with nature, objects and oneself. Interculturality is a way of bringing various visions to the world. Taking these insights into account, this book delivers three main takeaways:

- the authors do not have finite answers only temporary answers that need constant reappraisal and refinement,
- interculturality cannot be defined; it is all about what it means to you and what you see through its lenses and
- look elsewhere to move forward since the mainstream may have reached its limits and it is living in its rubbles – as soon as an idea becomes 'mainstream', step back, move *to and fro* (Dervin & R'boul, 2022).

We invite the readers to write some fragments as well; take up the habit of writing one fragment each day and let it sink, then come later and look at it more closely until it looks back at you; do not be quick to edit your fragments until you can recall the rationales behind them; focus on what has been said rather on what you want to say at that moment since you are probably reading the output of one of your selves. We all need to remember, as much cliché as it may sound, that the process of making sense of interculturality constitutes continuous, incessant and unfinished business…

References

Barthes, R. (2020). *Roland Barthes by Roland Barthes*. New York: Vintage.
Beecher, H. W. (1869). *The Original Plymouth Pulpit: Sermons of Henry Ward Beecher in Plymouth Church, Brooklyn* (Vol. 1). Cleveland, OH: Pilgrim Press.Choukri, M. (2007). *For Bread Alone*. Telegram Books.
Dervin, F. (2022). *Interculturality in Fragments: A Reflexive Approach*. Singapore: Springer.
Dervin, F. (2023). *Communicating around Interculturality in Research and Education*. London: Routledge.
Dervin, F., & R'boul, H. (2022). *Through the Looking-Glass of Interculturality: Autocritiques*. Singapore: Springer.
Nin, A. (2017). *Trapeze: The Unexpurgated Diary of Anaïs Nin, 1947–1955*. Athens, OH: Ohio University Press.
O'Brien, T. (2009). *The Things They Carried*. New York: Houghton Mifflin Harcourt.
R'boul, H., & Dervin, F. (2023). *Intercultural Communication Education and Research: Reenvisioning Fundamental Notions* (1st ed.). London: Routledge.

Index

relevance 45, 53, 66, 67, 82, 85, 125
repetition 6, 7, 105, 151, 160
representation 4, 21, 61, 92, 138
representatives 57
reproduction 58
reputation 30, 118, 148
research 2, 5–10, 12–16, 19, 24–33,
        42, 44, 45, 59, 62, 65, 68, 71,
        75–81, 87, 88, 90, 93, 95, 97,
        98, 104, 108–110, 114, 115,
        117, 119–127, 130–133, 136,
        140–142, 145, 146, 148–153,
        156, 158, 160, 162
researcher 36, 75, 104, 122
resemblance 78
resistance 4, 22, 68, 148
resources 2, 31, 38, 47, 51, 61, 115
response 2, 68, 77
retaliation 103
rethinking 7
reticence 10
revamp 148
revelations 89
reverberations 26, 52
reverse 21, 67, 77
review 15, 126
reviewers 9, 14, 30
revolution 123
rhetorics 19, 60, 63, 66, 67, 103, 147,
        149
rigid 27, 157
rigorous 29, 30, 44, 145
rigour 17, 30, 34, 56, 66, 89
rituals 150
robustness 66
romanticism 63
romanticizing 66, 77
roots 35, 57
rubrics 57, 128

sabotage 96, 123
Saturnalia 141
saviour 56
scepticism 148
schizophrenia 19, 143
schizophrenics 55
scholars 6–8, 10, 13, 14, 16–20, 23,
        25, 27–33, 35, 38, 43, 45, 47,
        48, 52, 57, 59, 60, 63–66, 70,
        71, 73, 74, 77, 78, 88–90, 92,
        99, 100, 103, 105, 108, 120,
        122–124, 126, 127, 140, 141,
        148, 156, 157, 161

scholarships 10, 14, 23, 25, 28, 31, 33,
        38, 43, 53, 56, 59, 65, 70, 76,
        82, 90, 91, 96, 99, 105, 131,
        147, 149, 151, 152
science 16, 30, 33, 36, 61, 67, 77, 93,
        104, 140
seismograph 130
self-actualizing 46
self-alterity 158
self-complacent 144
self-conscious 140
self-construction 144
self-critique 13, 70, 79, 102, 141, 157
self-doubt 147
self-examination 141
selfishness 80
self-projection 54
self-racializing 86
self-sufficient 86
sense 10, 11, 14, 16, 19, 20, 22, 23, 27,
        35, 36, 42, 46, 48, 50, 51, 53,
        59, 65–67, 70, 73, 77, 78, 84,
        87–89, 92, 94, 95, 99, 102, 103,
        110, 112, 114, 124, 128, 133,
        134, 140, 141, 143, 147, 148,
        150, 157, 158, 161, 162
sentiments 19, 62, 156
seriousness 77
shackles 10, 103
shortcomings 82
sight 18, 48
significance 39, 51, 86, 111
silences 7, 123
simplex 108, 109, 115, 132, 134, 139,
        150
simplexities 100, 106, 107, 112
simplicity 37, 106
singularity 58
Sisyphean 65
situated 13, 21, 44, 51, 65, 77, 78, 102,
        116, 123
sketch 70
skewed 17, 25, 64, 77, 143
sleepwalk 87
slogans 25, 35, 38, 94, 111, 145, 152,
        153
slogan-word 111
smokescreen 16, 17, 67
social 5, 8, 11, 14, 15, 20, 36, 39, 41,
        43, 44, 49, 51, 53, 56, 57, 59,
        66–68, 70, 72–75, 78, 103, 104,
        107, 121, 125, 126, 129, 139,
        142, 147, 152, 154, 158, 159

For Product Safety Concerns and Information please contact our EU
representative GPSR@taylorandfrancis.com
Taylor & Francis Verlag GmbH, Kaufingerstraße 24, 80331 München, Germany

www.ingramcontent.com/pod-product-compliance
Lightning Source LLC
Chambersburg PA
CBHW061738270326
41928CB00011B/2292